Roots and Branches

Roots & Branches

Grounding Religion in Our Human Experience

KENNETH R. OVERBERG, S.J.

Nihil Obstat: Rev. Nicholas Lohkamp, O.F.M
Rev. John. J. Jennings

Imprimi Potest: Rev. Jeremy Harrington, O.F.M.
Provincial

Imprimatur: +James H. Garland, V.G.
Archdiocese of Cincinnati
December 8, 1987

Scripture texts used in this work are taken from the *New American Bible,* copyright ©1970 by the Confraternity of Christian Doctrine, Washington, D.C., and are used by permission of the copyright owner. All rights reserved.

Book design by Julie Lonneman

Cover design by David Diehl

ISBN 0-86716-077-2

To
Ruth Graf, R.S.M.
and
Frank Brennan, S.J.

Foreword

"**Y**ou folks ought to take your show on the road! Teach this course in the parishes—that's where it's really needed." This is not an unusual comment about the Introduction to Theology course required at Xavier University. It is often made by a "nontraditional" student, one who is older and has returned to college.

The course has succeeded in generating interest in religion and theology among students previously less than enthusiastic about the subject. We who have taught the course many times recognize that it is most effective for the older students, those who have a greater variety of experiences to reflect upon. So, once again, the students taught the teachers—and this exploration of religion and human experience came into being.

Roots and Branches addresses a real need in today's Church. While there are many resources for considering Scripture and spirituality, few deal with the foundations of religion and religious experience. This book therefore aims to help all types of persons to ponder basic questions about life: Is there meaning in life? Is God real? What is religion and how does it fit into life?

If you are looking for a follow-up to parish programs such as RENEW and Christ Renews His Parish, this reflection on human experience and religious tradition will provide insight into the meaning and purpose of religion and also introduce the basic content and method of theology. But this book is also very appropriate for those who feel alienated from religion, or for those who simply have a vague sense of searching for something more.

Roots and Branches can be used in a variety of ways. If you choose reading and pondering alone, built-in pauses for reflection will help you apply the material to your own life. The book is also suitable for group study and discussion (the six chapters nicely fit a Lenten program). Points for discussion are given at the end of each chapter, and your group can certainly incorporate their more personal reflections into the discussion.

Acknowledgments

This small book, based on Xavier's course, accordingly owes much to all the faculty members who first shaped and then revised it again and again. I would also like to thank Eunice Staples, Bob Flack, S.J., Ruth Graf, R.S.M., Mary Humbert, S.C., Karen Hurley, Bill King, S.J., and Barbara Sheehan, S.P., for their help in preparing this book. Finally, a word of thanks to Xavier University for the grant which allowed me the time for writing.

Contents

INTRODUCTION
The Banyan Tree   1

CHAPTER ONE
New Roots: Searching for Something More   7

CHAPTER TWO
Tilling: Interpreting Human Experience   29

CHAPTER THREE
Some Branches: Appreciating Symbols and Stories   43

CHAPTER FOUR
Old Roots: Focusing on Moses and Jesus   63

CHAPTER FIVE
More Branches: Understanding Organized Religion   83

CHAPTER SIX
Pruning: Choosing Renewal and Growth   103

EPILOGUE
Theology: Developing New Branches   127

Bibliography   131

The Banyan Tree

R eligion is ambiguous. Maybe you have heard comments such as the following from your friends or children. Maybe you have voiced—or thought them yourself:

> "Religion is just a waste. It doesn't touch what's happening in my life."
>
> "How can there be a God when there is so much evil in the world?"
>
> "Marx and Freud were right. Religion is an escape. People create God because they can't face life."

Or perhaps your experience is quite different. Religion has been very important in your life. Your relationship with God has been nurtured by religious symbols and rituals. You desire to develop your spiritual life even more and to be more actively involved in your parish. Perhaps you have already participated in some form of renewal program where concerned people have shared not only their time but also themselves. Still, you sense that something is missing and you ask:

> "Where do we go next?"
>
> "How can we deepen our appreciation of our spiritual life?"

1

These two sets of questions and perceptions reflect very different experiences of life and religion and God. Yet, curiously, they all focus on the same cluster of issues:

Is there any meaning in life? Or is it just absurd?

Is God real? Or has the human family made up its God-stories in order to deal with life's difficulties?

What is religion and how does it fit into life?

Do the symbols and gestures of the Mass and other religious practices express an authentic faith in God? Or are they just empty symbols?

Most of us have been *given* answers to these questions. That may be the heart of the problem! We have been given answers—often from the earliest years of our lives—to questions we never had. For some these answers are sufficient. But for many of us, these answers finally do not work, often because they are not really *our* answers. Whether we are confronted with tragedy or doubt or absurdity, or whether we are searching for deeper meaning in an already positive experience, we sense a need for "something more."

The purpose of this book is to assist in that search for something more. It also provides suggestions on how to claim as truly your own the insights into those basic questions religious tradition offers.

In Chapter 1 you will be invited to reflect upon your own experience, to become aware of the deeper dimensions of your life. You will be encouraged to look into your ordinary human experience—friendship, nature, tragedy, love—and to see if you have experienced the divine in those very realities. Through this process, possible answers to life's questions will emerge—not as something imposed from without but as a reality rooted in your own life.

Then you will be challenged to look into religion. For the experience of God is found not only in friendship, nature, tragedy and love. Throughout history people have also experienced God in the practice of organized religion. All too often religion seems to be removed from the immediacy of everyday human experience. Yet many people claim religion to be a privileged place to encounter God. Why is this claim made? What connection is there between ordinary experiences and religion?

Chapter 2 explores the basis for this claim from two different perspectives: philosophy and theology. Chapter 3 provides insight into the language people use to express religious experiences: sign, symbol, parable and myth.

Against this backdrop Chapter 4 looks at the lives of two people, Moses and Jesus. Their lives, much like our own, were also special in that they led to the formation of new religions. By examining the movement from personal experience to organized religion among their followers, we can gain some insight into the purpose of religion and into the relationship between everyday experience and organized religion.

Tracing this movement from experience to religion in Chapter 5 will reveal the central role of community: the Jewish people with Moses and the disciples with Jesus. These followers of Moses and Jesus wanted to keep alive the vision and insight and personal experiences of Moses and Jesus. Through the remembering and handing on of these experiences, the formation of a religion spontaneously occurs. Thus the community serves as an essential bridge between experience and religion. (Because many of us are shaped by our North American emphasis on the *individual* person, we will have to make an extra effort to appreciate fully the significance of the community.)

But the existence of a community with its organization and structures also raises serious questions:

Is a community faithful in what it passes on? Or does it pass on only what serves its purposes?

Is organized religion really necessary? Hasn't too much havoc been raised throughout history in the name of religion?

How can religion keep from slipping into superstition?

Organized religion seems necessary and good, but also ambiguous and dangerous. Chapter 6 highlights this ambiguity and points to the need for continual reform and renewal in order to get back to the true purpose of religion: the remembering and handing on of the foundational values, insights and experiences. This ambiguity and this need for continual renewal lead us back to where we began: our own experience—and the all-too-common experience of religion's limits.

An Image for the Search

The fascinating banyan tree provides an excellent image for us in our search for something more—and for the process of this book. As it grows, this remarkable tropical tree not only develops branches like any other tree, it also drops new roots from its branches. These roots in turn become new trunks. The process goes on and on—new branches, new roots, new trunks, then more new branches. Some banyan trees are large enough to occupy an entire city block. People can walk through the maze of roots and branches as if the single tree were an entire forest.

We who are products of a religious tradition are like the banyan tree's new roots. Perhaps we are still dangling from the branches, not yet rooted. Or perhaps our experience has been very positive and our roots are solidly planted in good soil. We are becoming new trunks, supporting older branches and developing new branches of our own as we hand on our faith.

But whether still dangling or firmly rooted, we are dependent. The faith has been handed on to us; we have been and are still nurtured by other people and by a tradition with rituals and stories. These rituals and stories are the older branches of our banyan tree. They, of course, come from still older roots. Think of some of the "giants" of our history: Ignatius Loyola, Teresa of Avila, Francis of Assisi, Augustine. But even these older roots are dependent on still older branches: older traditions and Scripture itself. Finally we reach our original root and trunk: Jesus of Nazareth. And this Christian banyan tree is related to and originally dependent on

4

the Jewish banyan tree, for we can only understand Jesus if we understand his Jewish experience of God and life.

Undoubtedly, there are people who would prefer simply to ignore this banyan tree, to pretend that it really doesn't exist. There are others who feel separated from the tree, cut off by their own or others' actions. Still others may acknowledge some connection, but just take this bond for granted. Yet the banyan tree invites inspection by all—those who are disenchanted, those who are questioning, those who are searching for something more.

So let us enjoy the exploration of our banyan tree. Let's walk through the maze of roots and branches, carefully studying as many connections as possible. First, we turn to our ordinary lives and try to see the value of these dangling new roots: the richness and significance of our day-to-day living.

CHAPTER ONE

New Roots:
Searching for Something More

"It goes so fast...I didn't realize. So all that was going on and we never noticed," says Emily in Thorton Wilder's play, *Our Town*. Life is so fast-paced and so full of activities, "We don't have time to look at one another."

Indeed, so much is going on! For many of us, life is very full, at times even overwhelming. We have responsibilities for children, ourselves and perhaps elderly parents. Career pressures and financial worries can often oppress. Personal relationships, while nurturing, can also be a strain. World affairs stagger our imaginations: violence, starvation, the threat of nuclear holocaust.

Looking at that whirl of events, responsibilities, gifts, and frustrations, what can we say about life? *Is there more than meets the eye?*

The Givens of Life

We find ourselves already in the midst of our lives. It is as though we have been thrown into life without any choice. We have no control over our beginnings—our parents, our circumstances, our times—and little control over our end. We are plunged into the busy, wonderful, confusing reality we call life. This amazing kaleidoscope revolves in four concentric circles: ourselves, our personal relationships, society, the cosmos. To grasp the significance of our experiences, we must take time to reflect on our lives, to realize some of what is going on. Let's begin simply by looking at these four aspects of our everyday lives.

Self

We reflect upon what is happening in our lives. We ask ourselves questions which range from the very practical ("Why did I get a headache from last night's party?") to the very profound ("Why is there so much suffering in the world?"). We carry on dialogues with ourselves, over the ordinary (which ice cream to buy) or the significant (the morality of our business practices), and all in a very normal, nonschizophrenic way. As far as we know, we are the only animals with this capacity to stop and think about food, about sex, about the meaning of all our actions and of life itself. We are reflective; life's experiences develop, in part, within our own selves.

Family and Friends

A second aspect of life is all the people in our lives. Who we are and what we do are profoundly influenced by those people who are closest to us, our families and friends. They are a source of much happiness and much disappointment. Most of us experience our families as a mixture of good and bad, of that which promotes our growth as healthy human beings and that which hinders that growth. The percentage of good and bad varies tremendously, of course. And life often does not seem fair. We find ourselves with *this* family and must gradually learn to do the best with what has been given.

We have more choice in our friends. But even with friends, our experience is checkered: There is disappointment as well as wonderful nurturing. Promises are sometimes broken and hopes destroyed, but at other times we experience ourselves as loved, as having lasting value; we recognize that we too can love and make true commitments.

This give-and-take between ourselves and our families and friends leads us to appreciate essential aspects of what it means to be human.

Society

   More and more we learn how much society, its customs and institutions determine the contours of our lives. Consider for a moment the effect the media, business, government and religion have on 20th-century culture in the United States. The advertising industry tells us what to wear, what to buy and—much more importantly—what "really" constitutes human worth. Movies, television and music powerfully communicate their messages about success, power, pleasure and other fundamentals of life in a consumer society. Corporate influence extends around the globe, determining economic policies and even controlling the destinies of Third World countries. Government's decisions touch our lives from the smallest detail on package warning labels to weapons which threaten the very existence of the human family.

   Religion is another institution which greatly influences the lives of many people. Its impact is both positive and negative: It provides guidance and imposes guilt; nourishes life and stunts growth; offers wisdom and encourages immaturity. It has developed humanizing rituals and prophetic scriptures and lapsed into superstition and magic. It has challenged governments and cultures to act justly and colluded with oppressors.

   So pervasive is the power of society in media, industry, government and religion that our lives cannot avoid its overwhelming influence whether for good or evil. But before we worry about the good or evil, we must first recognize and acknowledge society's influence.

Cosmos

   Our life experience is also molded by our relationship with the cosmos. Our personalities and perspectives are affected by weather and landscape. We have gained understanding and much control over nature, yet we also recognize both the limits of our power and the ways we still remain dependent. In recent years the environmental crisis has reinforced all these insights and raised serious questions about our responsibilities for our planet.

   This, then, is the stuff of our lives, the back-and-forth

flow between ourselves and others, society's institutions, the whole cosmos. This is our life experience.

But is this all? Are we aware of anything else? Do we experience something more?

The Experience of 'Something More'

The work of psychologist Abraham Maslow helps us to answer these questions. Maslow believed that psychological theory had centered so much on neurotic experience that it had missed the insight to be gained from studying the experiences of healthy people. The most intense of these experiences he called "peak experiences." He found these to be basically the same as what have traditionally been called "religious experiences."

Characteristics of Peak Experiences

Through his investigations, Maslow gathered a list of characteristics of these peak experiences. Since Maslow's insights may help us appreciate more fully our own experiences, let's look at some of these characteristics, described in his book *Religion, Values and Peak Experiences*.

A central dimension of a peak experience is frequently the sense that *the whole world is unified and has meaning*. Just for a moment everything makes sense and fits together. Again we are not talking about an abstract, philosophical acceptance, but what Maslow calls a "clear perception." There is a profound recognition of the goodness of life. Even evil is accepted and understood as part of a larger whole. Chaos and absurdity do not have the final word. Evil does not undermine the basic goodness and meaningfulness of life. Profound fears, even of death, tend to disappear. Clearly, such an experience can have a lasting impact on how one views and lives life. Maslow claims such an experience permanently cured one of his subjects from chronic anxiety.

Another characteristic of the peak experience is its *unselfish nature*: It catches a person up in another object or person. The other object or person receives full attention and is appreciated in its own uniqueness. It is perceived as having its own independent reality; it is an end in itself and not merely a means. The person becomes self-forgetful and unselfish, accepting the other as worthwhile and valuable in itself. As an example, Maslow speaks of the mother examining in loving ecstasy every detail of her newborn infant from little toes to fingers!

Related to this characteristic are several others. The first is a *lack of consciousness of time and space*. The person is so caught up, so enthralled as to catch a glimpse of eternity. A minute may seem like a day or a year; the sense of being located in a particular place is lost. A second is *greater passivity and receptivity*. Because the other (person or thing) is affirmed as valuable in itself, the person is more ready to listen and receive. The third is *an enhancement of personal qualities*: The person becomes more loving and more accepting. Because differences and conflicts are resolved, greater acceptance and unity result and the individual moves more closely to his or her true identity. In general, people become more responsible, active and creative; they search for ways to reach out to others, to improve society, to do something good for the world.

Another characteristic of the peak experience is the *sense of gratitude*. The experience itself is recognized as gift, not something deserved. And so the person, feeling fortunate or graced, is moved to thank fate or to give praise to God. Gratitude, as experienced by the religious person, leads naturally to worship, praise and commitment.

The peak experience is also felt to be *self-validating*. Therefore, even though ambiguous and open to various interpretations, it is affirmed by the person as having intrinsic value and meaning. The experience justifies itself, "proves" itself—even though no scientific proof is possible. The danger here, Maslow warns, is that the person may be tempted to become antirational, refusing to admit that such experiences may be illusions. Thus, we need critical reflection on experience, acknowledging both the self-validating dimension and the possibility of fooling ourselves.

In his investigations Maslow also discovered people who could not report any peak experiences. At first he thought there were simply two groups: those who had peak experiences and those who did not. As his investigation continued, however, he found more and more who acknowledged such experiences. This gradually, led Maslow to conclude that the "non-peakers" were those who were afraid of such experiences, who denied them or turned away from them. He eventually compiled a list of characteristics of these non-peakers. They typically attempt to live in a completely rational or materialistic way. Peak experiences are equated with a loss of control or irrational behavior—and so to be rejected. Non-peakers likewise manifest a desperate need for control, an obsessive-compulsive fear of emotion, an ultra-scientific mentality which denies anything that is not logical, or an extremely practical, means-oriented perspective (peak experiences "earn no money, bake no bread"). Given the positive benefits of peak experiences, Maslow judged the non-peaker to be severely limited in both personal growth and personal fulfillment.

Peak Experiences and Religion

While Maslow's characteristics may help us clarify our own religious experiences, we must recall that Maslow took a very critical stance toward religion.

Maslow was working as a psychologist. He judged these types of experiences to be perfectly natural and human—and therefore open to psychological examination. He felt that experiences which were explainable only in supernatural terms in the past could now be investigated by science.

He contrasted the personal illumination of a sensitive prophet (the peak experience) with the conservative legalism of the religious organizational official. The contrast was severe!

In a peak experience, the prophet discovers new truth about self, the world and God. Maslow stressed the individuality of the experience, calling it "totally private" and hardly able to be shared. As a result, each person has his or her own private religion, with private symbols and rituals.

On the basis of this experience, nevertheless, an organization is built—in order to make the experience available to others. Thus begins the effort to translate into words, symbols and rituals the prophet's original experience. Maslow saw this as an attempt to communicate peak experiences to non-peakers, often by non-peakers themselves (that is, by those loyal to the organization but without a sense of the experience). The result, Maslow concluded, was the loss of the original experience and its replacement by words and statues and ceremonies which themselves come to be considered sacred. In a word, organized religion quickly slips into idolatry.

(It should be noted that in later writings, Maslow moved back somewhat from his harsh criticism of religion in *Religion, Values and Peak Experiences*. He recognized the dangers of too much concentration on one's own peak experiences and acknowledged that a person can become too individualistic, neglecting the need for others and for organized religion.)

Maslow was convinced of the basic split between peakers and non-peakers. In fact, he judged this split to be much more significant than other differences such as whether the experience was expressed in a theistic context or in a non-theistic one. The peak experience is shared by all the great world religions, such as Buddhism, Judaism and Christianity. Maslow went so far as to say that there are really only two religions: that of peakers and that of non-peakers.

Maslow's Contribution

What do Maslow's insights contribute to our questions about the "something more" in life? First, Maslow's extensive study helps to demonstrate the reasonableness of experiences which point to something more. From his psychological perspective, Maslow would judge that having such an experience is not contrary to healthy, human living; just the opposite, for peak experiences lead people to growth and fulfillment. Peakers have a better sense of their identity, are more loving and creative, and search for ways to improve the world. Having peak experiences is not contrary to reason, but a significant step toward true human identity.

But notice what Maslow is *not* saying. He is not saying that these experiences prove God's existence; remember that Maslow felt peak experiences could be expressed both in a theistic context and in a non-theistic one. Thus Maslow's work does not necessarily make a statement about God.

Likewise, Maslow does not prove any basis in reality for

the existence of peak experiences, although his work does add to the credibility of such occurrences in ordinary life. In other words, Maslow provides additional evidence that we are not simply fooling ourselves when we point to our peak experiences.

A second contribution which Maslow's work makes is the analysis of the experience and the description of its characteristics. Such descriptions can help us as we attempt to clarify our own experiences, or even help us to identify experiences which we have ignored or passed over. These descriptions also reveal the shared qualities of human living—our experiences are uniquely our own and yet similar to those of others.

Third, Maslow's perspective reminds us of the ambiguity of peak experiences. They are open to various interpretations. Serious people, even those who accept the reality of such events, may still differ in their judgments about them. For example, Maslow did not think they necessarily point to the existence of God. And similar experiences can be expressed in different religions: Buddhism, Christianity, Islam. This ambiguity, therefore, invites both careful analysis of the experience in order to avoid illusion and a certain tolerance which acknowledges that serious and sensitive persons may describe and embody their peak experiences in a variety of ways.

Pause and reflect on your own experience. Can you remember any moments in your life which Maslow would describe as peak experiences?

Encountering God

Thus, throughout its history, the human family has been challenged by life to ask basic questions: What does it all mean? Where is it all going? What am I all about? Is there something more? And throughout its history, the human family has found insight into these questions through peak experiences.

Answers have varied tremendously. But in many cultures and in many different times and places, humans have insisted that there is meaning in life, that there is something more than just the confusing kaleidoscope of ourselves and others and the cosmos. This "something more" has been named in many ways; many peoples have called this reality "god."

Those of us in the Judeo-Christian tradition have come to believe that there is only one God. The Jews' experience of life led them to this conviction and to the unique belief that this one God was active in their history, freeing them from slavery and choosing them as God's own people. Jesus called this God "Abba" ("Daddy") and taught his disciples about Abba's Reign. The disciples came to recognize that in Jesus they had met God, that Jesus was God. Gradually the Christian belief in the Trinity was articulated: that there is one God who is Father, Son and Spirit.

Thus for Jew and Christian, life's experience points to something more. God, this tradition claims, is the source and goal of all life; indeed, God provides the final answer to what life is all about.

But where is this God in our experience of life? How do we know as surely as the Jews and Christians before us that there really is something more? Most of us first agreed to God's existence because we were told about God as children. We were told to believe. On others' word, we accepted that God existed, that God loved us and that God made sense out of our life. But where did that answer first come from? And is another's word still enough? Does belief in God make sense in our life now?

Many people affirm their belief in God by pointing to their peak experiences, to the experiences in their lives where they have become aware of something more. They find God not "out there" somewhere, but within the events—often ordinary events—of life. They experience God as another dimension of that flow back and forth with the circles of self, relationships, society and the cosmos. Some examples will help us to clarify the meaning of this type of experience.

The Experience of Nature

One very common setting for experiencing God is nature. We don't have to be poets to get caught up in the beauty of sunsets, the power of oceans, the majesty of mountains. In pondering the awesomeness of creation, people have claimed to be aware of God. This is not the same as rationalizing how there must be some "first cause" or creator. Rather, a feeling bubbles up from within and leads the person to affirm that there *must* be something more—not because science demands it, not because the Bible says so, but because the experience itself points to this other dimension.

This close tie between reverence for nature and the experience of God can be seen throughout the writings of French scientist Pierre Teilhard de Chardin, S.J. Even as a child, Teilhard was enchanted with rocks and minerals, insects and wildflowers. Such enchantment led not only to doctoral studies and a career in geology and paleontology but also to a profound sense of nature as a source of revelation. This sense is clearly expressed in Teilhard's "Hymn to Matter":

> Blessed be you, harsh matter, barren soil, stubborn rock: you who yield only to violence, you who force us to work if we would eat.
>
> Blessed be you, perilous matter, violent sea, untameable passion: you who unless we fetter you will devour us.
>
> Blessed be you, mighty matter, irresistible march of evolution, reality ever new-born; you who, by constantly shattering our mental categories, force us to go ever further and further in our pursuit of the truth.
>
> Blessed be you, universal matter, immeasurable time, boundless ether, triple abyss of stars and atoms

and generations: you who by overflowing and dissolving our narrow standards or measurement reveal to us the dimensions of God....I acclaim you as the divine milieu. (*Hymn of the Universe*)

The Experience of Love and Friendship

Another typical experience which opens up a deeper dimension of everyday life is love and friendship. People in love give and receive affirmation which has nothing to do with what they deserve. Instead, life is experienced as gift. Their love seems to be surrounded by an endless love. This experience of something more is found in different kinds of love: the depth of love between wife and husband, the wonder of a parent's love for a child, the steadfast love of true friends. In different contexts of love, people are led to profess: "There must be a God." The statement cannot be proved scientifically, the individual just *knows* it to be true.

Even in the horror of a concentration camp, Victor Frankl could be assured of the reality of something more just by the memory of his beloved wife:

A thought transfixed me: for the first time in my life I saw the truth as it is set into song by so many poets, proclaimed as the final wisdom by so many thinkers. The truth—that love is the ultimate and the highest goal to which man can aspire. Then I grasped the meaning of the greatest secret that human poetry and human thought and belief have to impart: *The salvation of man is through love and in love.* I understood how a man who has nothing left in this world still may know bliss, be it only for a brief moment, in the contemplation of his beloved. In a position of utter desolation, when man cannot express himself in positive action, when his only achievement may consist in enduring his sufferings in the right way— an honorable way—in such a position man can, through loving contemplation of the image he carries of his beloved, achieve fulfillment. For the first time in my life I was able to understand the meaning of the words, "The angels are lost in perpetual contemplation of an infinite glory."

(Man's Search for Meaning)

Although his life experience was very different than Frankl's, Thomas Merton also found love to be a source of revelation:

We exist solely for this, to be the place He has chosen for His presence, His manifestation in the world, His epiphany....[I]f we once began to recognize, humbly but truly, the real value of our own self, we would see that this value was the sign of God in our being, the signature of God upon our being. Fortunately, the love of our fellow man is given us as the way of realizing this....It is the love of my lover, my brother or my child that sees God in me, makes God credible to myself in me. And it is my love for my lover, my child, my brother, that enables me to show God to him or her in himself or herself. Love is the epiphany of God in our poverty.

(The Message of Thomas Merton)

The Experience of the Need for Grace

The struggle for moral goodness serves as another example of how our everyday experiences reveal God's existence. Especially in moments of weakness or situations of limitations, people acknowledge an awareness of something more which empowers them. This "outside help" is often named grace. The experience is one of being lifted up, reborn, or even saved. Often we recognize this same reality in those we admire—the official or unofficial "saints."

This experience of grace can happen in the most ordinary of moments. A line from William Blake, "We are put on earth for a little space that we may learn to bear the beams of love," called to Dorothy Day's mind a bus ride:

Suddenly I remember coming home from a meeting in Brooklyn many years ago, sitting in an uncomfortable bus seat facing a few poor people. One of them, a downcast, ragged man, suddenly epitomized for me the desolation, the hopelessness of the destitute, and I began to weep. I had been struck by one of those "beams of love," wounded by it in a most particular way. It was my own condition that I was weeping about—my own hardness of heart, my own sinfulness. I recognized this as a moment of truth, an experience of what the *New Catechism* calls our "tremendous, universal, inevitable and yet inexcusable incapacity to love...."

Perhaps I knew in that moment in the bus in Brooklyn what St. Augustine meant when he cried out, "May I know myself so that I may know thee." Because I felt so strongly my nothingness, my powerlessness to do anything about this horrifying recognition of my own hardness of heart, it drove me to the recognition that in God alone was my strength. Without Him I could do nothing. Yet I could do all things in Him Who strengthened me. So there was happiness there, too. The tears were of joy as well as grief. (*By Little and By Little*)

The Experience of Tragedy

As the experience of weakness hints, not all experiences of God are rooted in joyful situations. Indeed, some of the most powerful insights into the presence of God in everyday life come from tragedies. Sickness and death can lead to despair and utter darkness. Yet, amazingly, such experiences can also open up life and even death to the Mystery which is in all and surpasses all. A person sits at a dying friend's bedside and stares into the abyss of death—and discovers there a loving Power, a holy Presence, which evokes trust and hope. A family grapples with the pain of bereavement—and they sense consolation even in the darkness. Grief does not tumble into despair; somehow the promise of new light and life flickers anew. Tragedy occurs in so many other ways, both in the lives of individuals and of entire peoples: separation and oppression; mental illness and terrorism; starvation and floods and threats of nuclear war. These events are overwhelming and yet, at times, grace-filled.

Argentine Adolfo Perez Esquivel, winner of the 1980 Nobel Peace Prize, was repeatedly thrown into prison because of his human rights activities. He describes his experience of liberation in oppression, of light in darkness, in this way:

> In La Plata Prison Adolfo was forbidden all books, even a Bible. Faced with long days and nights of solitude he had time to appreciate what he calls "God's silence"—the place where faith ripens. Here in prison, everything Adolfo had ever received in the way of Christian culture began to come back to him in an uninterrupted series of insights, at once familiar and fresh. A kind of spiritual nourishment took charge, and Adolfo found, for instance, that he could write out whole passages of the gospel by heart. Once more in the history of oppression, for Adolfo as for so many before and after him, the lethal experience of prison paradoxically became an experience of interior liberation—a kind of spiritual striking root. (*Christ in a Poncho*)

The Experience of Religion

Religion is another situation in which people claim to encounter God. The very purpose of religion is to remember special encounters with God and to help create the conditions in which God will be experienced again. Many people thus point to religion as a way to God, a setting in which Holy Mystery meets the person. Perhaps this meeting occurs in the quiet of a retreat or in the celebration of salvation history in the Easter vigil. Perhaps one experiences a forgiving God in the Sacrament of Reconciliation or proclaims God's love in marriage. In Roman Catholic practice, the sacraments celebrate the major moments of the life cycle and allow these moments to speak of something more, to point to Mystery present in all areas of life.

Yet for some people religion also has strong negative qualities. They find that religion has become boring routine.

They experience its archaic language and meaningless symbols and gestures as merely reinforcing the status quo of the religion's structures. Little in religion reminds them of those special encounters with God; little leads them to the experience of something more.

Even in the face of this ambiguity, many continue to claim that religion is a privileged place for the encounter with God. One dimension of religion which leads to an experience of God is community. By belonging to a community, by feeling part of its history and ideals, people come to an awareness of something more that is present within the community. Luis Espinal, S.J., who was assassinated for his human rights work in Bolivia, expresses the power and hope nurtured by his experience of the Christian religion in this Easter prayer:

> There are Christians
> who have hysterical reactions
> as if the world had slipped out of
> God's hands.
> They are violent
> as if they were risking everything.
> But we believe in history.
> The world is not a roll of the dice
> on its way toward chaos.
> A new world has begun to happen
> since Christ has risen....
> Jesus Christ,
> we rejoice in your definitive triumph....
> We march behind you on the road
> to the future.
> You are with us. You are our
> immortality....

The Experience of Struggling for Justice

Another communal setting for encountering God is the struggle for justice and freedom. Working and living with others leads people to recognize the fundamental human dignity of all persons—and the need for action to heal the afflicted and to change unjust structures of society. People have a sense of responsibility for other people. In the practical effort to bring about greater justice and liberation, they sense God calling them to this project and energizing their efforts.

Jean Vanier, founder of the L'Arche communities for people with handicaps, describes such an experience:

> I have learned more about the Gospels from handicapped people, those on the margins of our society, those who have been crushed and hurt, than I have from the wise and the prudent. Through their own growth and acceptance and surrender, wounded people have taught me that I must learn to accept my weakness and not pretend to be strong and capable. Handicapped people have shown me how handicapped I am, how handicapped we all are. They have reminded me that we are all weak and all called to death and that these are the realities of which we are most afraid. They have shown me how much I need Jesus the Healer. It is only when we accept these things that we can learn to open ourselves to the Spirit of love which Jesus promised us. Jesus came to give life and to give it abundantly. He calls us from death to life, for He, the Lamb of God, took death on Himself and conquered it. He came to preach good news to the poor, liberty to the oppressed and freedom to captives (cf. Luke 4, 18). Some of us are captives of our own misery and loneliness, others of false values and possessions; all of us are captives of our fear. Jesus came to free us all by the gifts of His Spirit and calls us to a new life of the Beatitudes and of community. (*Be Not Afraid*)

Pause and reflect on your own experience. Which of the experiences described above has given you the strongest sense of "something more"?

The Ambiguity of Experience

Experiences of God in nature or love or tragedy or religion have led people to search for appropriate expression and explanation of these ordinary yet extraordinary events. Poets and philosophers and theologians make use of images and symbols of wonder and awe, abstract explanations of Being and grace in an attempt to describe that which is finally beyond description. In our search for meaning such attempts at explanation are important; indeed, we will attempt this in the next chapter.

But for now, let us recall how Maslow described these experiences in which we find hints of something more.

First, *the experience of God is ambiguous*. The experience, though very powerful for the person involved, is open to other interpretations. These other interpretations may come from within ("Did I really experience God or am I just making it up, just fooling myself?") or from without ("Don't be naive; you're just pretending in order to get yourself through a painful time!"). Certainly Victor Frankl could have been accused of trying to avoid the dreadful reality of the concentration camp. But, as we just read in his comments on love, *he* was utterly convinced of the reality and significance of his experience.

Second, *we cannot make such experiences happen*. Instead, the experience just seems to happen to us. We can help create conditions that are conducive to such encounters with God—such as liturgies—but we cannot force them. We can take time off for a retreat or make time to pray in quiet away from the distractions and responsibilities and noise of everyday life. The quiet gives an opportunity to be attentive to the deeper dimensions of life, but quiet and attentiveness cannot make the experience happen. It simply comes to us, sometimes when we least expect it. So it was in Dorothy Day's experience. She became aware of her own weakness and of her need for God—while riding a bus!

Third, *such experiences are perceived as pure gift*. An experience of God is not a constant; we cannot hold on to it. It comes and goes in our lives. A person's encounter with God is an experience of receiving something; it is gift.

Fourth, *the experience comes from within and points beyond everyday life*. Peak experiences cannot be forced from above by some authority. As we have seen in the descriptions above, the encounter with God "bubbles up" from within and breaks into our consciousness. We become aware of the gift, and it leads us to recognize that there is something more than just ourselves and our world.

Fifth, *such experiences involve the whole person*. Meeting God through ordinary events of life is not just a head-trip, not just a philosophical exercise in which a person calmly analyzes life and moves step-by-step to a conclusion. Nor is it merely an emotion. It is, instead, a deeply personal encounter, an act of the whole person, head and heart, responding to God's initiative. Jean Vanier's reaction to those with handicaps clearly was neither merely to think about what he should do nor just to feel sorry for the people. In and through these people, Vanier encountered God in the depths of his being.

Finally, *these experiences are of great significance for people's lives*. What may appear ambiguous to the outsider is judged absolutely essential by the person involved. Such an experience opens up the deeper dimension of life, provides insight, hope and direction; it answers the fundamental questions about the meaning of life. The resultant hope, courage and commitment are evident in the lives of people like Thomas Merton and Dorothy Day.

The very ambiguity of these ordinary experiences which allows a glimpse of Mystery has led to much discussion and doubt. Serious and sensitive people question the authenticity of such claims, suggesting that wishing does not make it so. Authors such as Marx and Freud claim that religion's "illusions" have impaired human growth, both socially and individually.

These challenges must be taken seriously, for history demonstrates the many abuses of religion. There is sufficient historical evidence to show that Marx was correct in stating that people and governments have used religion to achieve their own goals, to promote their ideas, to stay in power, to oppress others. We have only to look around our world to see civil wars, persecution, terrorism—all in the name of religion. A closer look in such places as Latin America reveals religion's cooperation with the colonialism of past ages and its oppressive political structures. Even at home in the United States many are now working to change the second-class status of women and all laity in the Church.

Freud focused on the individual's abuse of religion: making God into a superhuman crutch to help people face the difficulties of life. Life is unfair, sometimes tragic. Freud saw religion's appeal to God as an inauthentic way of facing the dark side of life. God simply became a gigantic security blanket.

Undoubtedly Marx and Freud were right—in part! Religion has been abused: Religion has been used to keep people "in their place." Religion has been used to dull people's sensitivities to personal and social evil. Religion has been used as a convenient way out of coping with the difficult, the absurd. But many would claim that such abuse is not the whole story. Rather than proving the falseness of religion, such abuse calls for the need to consider carefully the meaning of religion and the need for reform and renewal when abuse is recognized.

Summing Up

Many who claim the authenticity of religion do so because of what others have experienced, or taught, or said. But, finally, such a claim must go back to one's own human experience, to the ordinary events in which God is revealed. Such experiences—and the religions in which they are expressed and for which they provide a foundation—must be held up against the counterclaims of a Marx or a Freud.

The difficulty, especially for our scientific mindset, is that such experiences are not subject to ordinary empirical verification. Microscopes and computers provide no help in describing and analyzing experiences of Mystery. Instead, we must learn to trust our own experiences—and also to test them. In the next chapter, with the help of philosophy and theology, we will attempt such analysis and interpretation.

But first, let's return to our image of the banyan tree. Recall how the tree grows: From its branches, new roots develop and drop down to the earth, very gradually forming new trunks. We are those aerial roots as we encounter God through the events of our everyday world.

Some new roots are barely budding, hardly emerging from the branch. For these people, faith is still very much what has been handed on; they affirm what has been given in their religion, but the affirmation is not really grounded in their own experience. Others are now dangling in mid-air, somewhat independent of the "mother branch," but still searching for soil to nourish this new life. These people may experience their faith in various ways. Some catch brief glimpses of the meaning of religion and sense the truth of these glimpses. Or they feel the uneasiness of a dangling root. They are not satisfied with memorized answers and creeds; question and doubt are their experience of religion.

Still others have already begun to implant in the earth. They recognize and accept the experiences which provide insight into the meaning and direction of living. They know God's presence and centrality and religion's role in expressing this mystery in and through the experiences. Some are solidly rooted and have become new trunks, sending out new branches, handing on the faith, celebrating God's reality.

Finally, to complicate the image, it seems important to note that each one of us is never completely identified with one particular stage of the banyan tree's growth. Few are fully integrated. Even the wise and holy probably find areas of life where they are still dangling.

For discussion or reflection:

1) What are your basic questions about life? What insights, fears or tensions do you bring to these questions? How is your questioning affected by the four concentric circles in which you live?

2) What experiences have given you or people you know the strongest sense of something more? Can you see effects in your life or the lives of these others in keeping with the characteristics of a peak experience Maslow describes?

3) *Would you identify yourself or anyone you know as a non-peaker? Why? Is this a cause for concern?*

4) *What has been your experience of religion? Does religion help or hinder your struggle with life's basic questions?*

5) *Based on this chapter and your own experience, would you identify peak experiences as religious experiences, as illusions or as something hard to categorize?*

CHAPTER TWO

Tilling:
Interpreting Human Experience

The experience of God is difficult to describe, even more difficult to explain. We cannot put our experiences of "something more" under a microscope; there is no scientific proof. Yet, we can point to such experiences, or at least listen to others' claims about such events. In this chapter, therefore, we will step back and reflect upon the experiences described in Chapter 1.

This reflection will help us interpret the experience and answer such questions as "What makes the experience of God, whether in nature or love or tragedy, possible?" and "Why do we have these experiences?" Even if reflection cannot *prove* the experience, it can show that such an experience is not unreasonable, not contrary to careful analysis or to common sense.

Our reflection will be based on two different perspectives: philosophical and theological. As we study these perspectives, we want to keep in mind our own experiences, trying to see if this theory enlightens the events of our lives.

A Philosophical Perspective

The thoughts of Maurice Blondel, a French philosopher who died in 1949, and Karl Rahner, the German Jesuit who died in 1984, provide the basis for a philosophical perspective. This analysis will answer the basic question: "Do I really experience

God or am I just making it up, just fooling myself?" As an aid in understanding the philosophical reflections, let's start with the conclusion and then carefully trace how Blondel and Rahner reach that conclusion.

What makes experiences of something more possible? Blondel and Rahner would answer simply: because we humans are built that way. That is, the very structure of human nature is to be open to and in relationship with something more (the philosopher will name this something more the Transcendent, the Infinite, Absolute Being). Just as we are social beings, built to be in relationships with other people, so too we are built to be in relationship with the Infinite (God). The potential is a given in our human nature. Fulfillment of our potential for human relationships depends both on others' initiative and our response. In the same way, our relationship with God depends on God's initiative and our response. But the possibility of such a relationship ought not to surprise us; it is an essential part of being human.

Blondel's 'Inexaustible Willing'

Blondel reached this conclusion by reflecting on human action. He focused in particular on willing and loving—the yearnings of the human heart. He was convinced that truth could be found by studying human life, history and experience. That is, living is prior to philosophizing.

So, if we study human living, what do we find? Blondel answered that we find a whole series of decisions and actions by which we shape our future and, indeed, our very selves. Quite simply, we are never a finished product. All of us can look back over our personal history and see how people and events have shaped us and how we participated in that process. Each of us can say at any particular moment, "I am this person with this history." At the same time, that's not all the "I" we will be. New people, new events, new choices, new actions will continually create a new "I." We remain who we are yet we change constantly. There is no way to avoid this process, for, as the cliche reminds us, not to choose is to choose. The person, the "I," is never fully realized.

Consider major decisions in your life: your choice to go

to college or not; your choice to marry or to remain single or to enter religious life; your choice about career and where to live; even your choice about how to deal with events that simply happened to you, such as an accident or sickness. All of these choices and the actions based on them helped to create the particular person you are. At no point in the process could you have said, "Well, that's it. I'm complete now. There's no need for future decisions and actions." Even in old age, choices remain. And, as we learn more about dying and death, we realize that even this final moment presents the option of denial or acceptance.

Such is the truth, the reality which Blondel discovered in his reflection on human living. In his language, human beings make choices and act in order to become more truly themselves. They realize that in some way they are not yet who they are meant to be; they must constantly strive to achieve this. Blondel claimed that there is thus an infinite distance between ourselves and the selves we are meant to be. We seek to fill in this distance, but we never fully succeed. Blondel named this striving "inexhaustible willing," a built-in thrust in the very core of our being toward something more.

In Blondel's analysis, this willing, this reaching with the heart, was found to be truly inexhaustible. The person's choices and concerns reach toward more and more people, and yet this drive is never fulfilled. Nothing in the world, no finite reality, is enough to satisfy. Blondel went on to claim that every human being therefore faces an inevitable option: to acknowledge this inexhaustible willing and so be open to the Infinite (for nothing finite is sufficient) or to deny this built-in drive and try to be satisfied with finite things.

Clearly, then, this option is fundamental. In making it, we determine who we will be. We either acknowledge our openness to the Infinite or we violate the thrust built into our nature, pretending that this dimension does not exist. For Blondel, this fundamental option does not have to be explicit, but can be part of other significant choices in which we express our values and commitments (e.g., to justice, fidelity, love). Thus a person can be open to the reality of God even if that person has never heard of God.

On the other hand, we can deny this built-in relatedness to God. We can invest the finite with infinite value. We might, for example, seek total fulfillment in money, power or pleasure. Blondel judged this fundamental option harshly, for such a choice condemns a person never to be who he or she is meant to be. Such a choice does violence to the structure of human nature and goes counter to one's own destiny. Blondel considered such a choice idolatry because it locks a person into the finite world.

Pause and reflect on your own experience. Consider the choices which have made you "more truly yourself." Do you see in them a pattern of reaching with your heart toward the Infinite?

Rahner's 'Unlimited Knowing'

Karl Rahner also reached the conclusion that human beings are built to be in relation with God. Rahner justified this view by a penetrating analysis of human knowledge.

Most of us take for granted what is involved in the process of knowing. One of the tasks of the philosopher is to sift through what we take for granted, to search for explanations for human activity. Thus the philosopher will ask, "How do we know that we know?" and "What is truth?" In this abstract but important analysis, Rahner uncovered fundamental implications built into our process of knowing.

Everything we know, Rahner pointed out, is limited, is a *particular* object: This is a book. That is a person. Something else is a tree. Everything we know has boundaries. But, at the same time that we recognize a boundary, we also implicitly realize that there is something beyond the boundary. To know a limit is already to be beyond the limit.

For example, look at the book in your hands. You see it to be a certain size. Beyond its limits is something else: your fingers, the room, the air. As you focus on the limits of the book, you acknowledge that there is something else beyond it.

Rahner took this commonsense insight and expanded it

to all that we know or can know. The dynamic is the same: We can know all finite things; but in saying this, we are already beyond all finite things. Thus, Rahner claimed, in the very process of knowing, the human mind always reaches beyond what it knows and strives for something more. Since our minds always move beyond all finite things, the only reality which can satisfy our striving is the Infinite.

Another way to try to grasp Rahner's insight is to look carefully at our language and its implications. To say, "This is a book," is to affirm implicitly that the book has existence. It *is*. But whenever we affirm that something exists, we also affirm its limitation. It is *this* or *that*; it is a specific object.

But the verb *is* is too big for any one particular thing. There is only one reality which is not limited, toward which our minds strive and about which we can simply say, "This reality is": the Infinite. Again, Rahner claimed that in affirming the existence of some limited reality we implicitly affirm the existence of infinite reality.

Notice that the dynamic is the same as Blondel's inexhaustible willing, except that Rahner focuses on the human *intellect*. Built into human nature is a movement toward something more. In every act of knowing we implicitly affirm the existence of a God. We do not know this God in the same way that we know all other realities. Rather, it is a built-in affirmation; God's existence makes our knowing possible. God is the goal toward which our minds strive. This striving is a given; but we must choose whether or not to acknowledge it in thought and action. As with Blondel, this choice is a fundamental option: to be open to the Infinite (and so acknowledge our true self) or to reject this dimension (and so violate the very structure of human nature).

Pause and reflect on your own experience. How and when have you experienced dissatisfaction with the finite, of wanting to know more, of striving for the Infinite?

A Theological Perspective

The psychological work of Maslow indicates that peak experiences are part of being human. The philosophical studies of Blondel and Rahner show that relationship with the Infinite (God) fits an understanding of the person which takes seriously both head and heart.

We can say that the human person is a finite being who has an infinite capacity. We feel made for something more, yet cannot reach our goal alone. If we are to satisfy our deepest human yearnings, then we must listen for some communication from the Infinite. With this consideration we move on to a theological perspective and an identification of religious experience as "revelation."

In and through ordinary events of life, people claim to experience God: to stand in awe of God's greatness, to enjoy God's love, to know God's healing grace. The contemporary American theologian Avery Dulles, S.J., analyzes this claim, attempting to focus on the theological dimension. Dulles demonstrates how this type of experience can rightly be called revelation. (See his "Revelation and Discovery" in *Theology and Discovery*, edited by William J. Kelly, S.J.)

Dulles noted that for many people the word *revelation* emphasizes knowledge freely given by God (that is, "the insertion of prefabricated divine thoughts"). This view of revelation, however, is not very helpful, for reflection shows that human inquiry and knowledge are always a part of the total experience. Prefabricated ideas cannot simply be poured into human brains. Dulles set out to develop a more nuanced understanding of revelation which would take seriously both God's activity and the human person's.

Dulles chose the model of scientific discovery to help in this task for three reasons: (1) to ensure that this new understanding of revelation would reflect the characteristics of human knowledge; (2) to suggest that revelation, like scientific discovery, represents a new advance in knowledge, something more than a mere application of previous knowledge; (3) to imply by the use of the word *discovery* that revelation involves an important insight that changes one's outlook. Dulles also stressed, however, that while the model of scientific discovery can help us to appreciate revelation, there is also a significant difference: In revelation, the person encounters God; there is a new and deeper relationship between God and the individual.

Dulles's Stages of Discovery

Dulles described four stages in the process of discovery. He then applied each to one's encounter with God:

The first stage is *preparation*; its key characteristic is puzzlement. Keen and curious scientific minds, aware of unanswered questions, seek solutions. They see not only the problem but also hints of a solution. They possess confidence that the problem can be solved, and so puzzlement leads to questioning and searching, not paralysis.

Likewise, those puzzling over the meaning of life experience ask themselves, "What's it all about?" Open to the possibility of something more, they pay attention to the events of their lives, searching to see if life is ultimately absurd or meaningful. They look for clues with a certain confidence that some insight can be found, even if everything cannot be finally proved.

Dulles claimed that this questioning and searching, this restlessness with life, is the result of the human spirit's attraction to God. He recalled Augustine's statement, "You have made us for yourself, O Lord, and our hearts are restless until they rest in you." Thus, hidden in the very beginnings of the process of revelation is the activity of God. What we may first name as our own search for meaning, our own puzzlement, is already God pulling us beyond ourselves. (The philosophical analysis of the previous section helps elucidate this divine attraction.)

The second stage of scientific discovery is *incubation*. Now the searching begins in earnest. Ransacking one's brains is the key characteristic at this stage. Data are collected. Clues are discovered and fitted together. Ideas pop into the mind. Various possibilities arise and are checked out. There may even be a sense of anticipation, of being on the edge of a new discovery.

So, too, in the religious experience of revelation. The individual turns toward God, asking for light and help. Ransacking one's brains is again the key, only here one looks for hints of God's presence—in nature, in history, in personal experiences. This is a time for searching for clues.

Dulles warns that we cannot force the evidence to speak to us. And this is an important warning, for while our activity is important, it is not sufficient. God must also be involved. The process is not under our own control. We must search, but we must also wait attentively.

Illumination is the third and climactic stage in scientific discovery. Insight is the key characteristic. The solution is found; the new discovery is made! Surprisingly, this insight often comes when we least expect it. Suddenly the pieces just fit together, often during a period of rest or quiet and not in the concentration of the search.

The same dynamic is present in revelation. Many religions use the symbol of light, of illumination, to describe this breakthrough event. Life is understood in a new way; God is experienced in a new depth. As in scientific discovery, the moment often comes in a time of quiet. Thus all traditions describe "mountaintop" or "desert" experiences. But it can also come in the midst of life (recall Dorothy Day's experience while riding a bus).

Yet the process does not stop at this climactic point. Insight is not sufficient; the task remains to check out the truthfulness of this new insight. *Confirmation*, then, is the fourth and final step in discovery.

Confirmation is essential because of the possibility of illusion, but it is also very difficult to achieve. The discovery implies grasping the not-yet-known. It is a leap forward, a leap not necessarily shared by others (who may reject the new insight). A discovery frequently cannot be expressed or confirmed by old categories and methods; a new view is therefore required to appreciate it.

Dulles suggested three criteria which can help to confirm a discovery. The first is *coherence*: The insight fits with what was previously anticipated. The second is *persuasiveness*: The discovery explains more things in a better way. The third is *acceptability to others*: The discovery is confirmed as other serious, careful people accept it and provide support for the discoverer.

In the experience of revelation there is an equal need for confirmation. We have already described the ambiguity of peak experiences, which are open to a variety of interpretations and subject to the risk of illusion. The need to check out one's experience is clear. And confirmation is probably even more difficult in the area of religion.

As we have seen earlier, God's existence cannot be proved. The believer will point to an experience of God; the unbeliever will speak of fate or chance or illusion. A new view is necessary; this new view can rightly be called a conversion.

The same three criteria can be used to show that a religious discovery is reasonable:

Coherence means that our experience of God somehow fits with our anticipation, with the clues we found along the way. Again, Dulles referred to Augustine who stated that when we meet God, we find that in some sense we have already known God.

The religious discovery—or revelation—gives light to our living; it is more *persuasive*. The events of love and tragedy are experienced in a larger context; the mystery of life is seen and accepted; meaning, not absurdity, is seen as the foundation and future of all life.

Finally, this view of reality is *shared by others*. The person who experiences the divine seeks to express this good news. There is joy in the discovery and a desire to reach out and share it with others.

Pause and reflect on your own experience. How many of Dulles's four stages of discovery (revelation) can you trace in your own life?

Revelation as Relationship

Dulles contrasted his model of revelation as discovery with the older model of revelation as classroom instruction. The older description of revelation clearly stressed both the interpersonal character of revelation and the divine authority (God was the professor). But, just as in some classrooms all the activity is the professor's while the students just sit and listen, so too in revelation the older model stressed God's action but the human role was much too passive.

In the discovery model, however, humans are clearly very active, questioning, searching, coming to insights, seeking confirmation. The disadvantage of the newer analogy is that God's activity may be missed. This is why Dulles emphasized that God is present from the beginning—even in the preparation/puzzlement stage. What looks like merely human questioning is in fact God drawing and attracting the person toward the fullness of life.

God does not have to break into the human world in the dramatic ways sometimes depicted in Hollywood's biblical movies. Rather, because God is immanent as well as transcendent, the Divine can also work gently from within all creation—including human beings.

Dulles therefore defined revelation as "the process by which God, working within human history and human tradition, enables his spiritual creatures to discern more profoundly the true meaning of their existence." Dulles also emphasized that revelation does not include just *ideas about* God. Revelation is indeed an *encounter with* God. This encounter takes place through the mediation of other objects and events; that is, we experience God in love or nature or tragedy or religion. We do not see God face-to-face, yet this is truly a person-to-person relationship.

In this relationship God takes the initiative, Dulles insists, like Blondel and Rahner before him. Human beings feel made for something more and are directed toward the Infinite, but they are unable to grasp God by themselves. The first step is God's, although this gentle attraction may be difficult to discern in the events of life. God's *initiative* invites the person's *response*.

Before ending our theological reflection on the experience of God, we must briefly consider the human response of openness and affirmation called *faith*. The person says yes to the divine initiative, to this person-to-person relationship. This yes is an expression of the whole person, a true commitment and acceptance.

The response of faith will be expressed in various ways, depending on the "clues" used to discover God's invitation. One who has been moved by the power or beauty of nature will probably affirm God's existence as the All-Powerful One or as Creator. If God has been encountered in suffering or as the infinite goal of one's heart and mind, then faith will speak of God as Holy Mystery. The person who rejoices in being alive and has met God in love and friendship, will affirm God as Love.

Whatever name is used to describe God, most religious traditions—certainly Judaism and Christianity—say that God is a personal being. This does not mean, of course, that God is just like us. It does mean that the fundamental qualities we experience in each other must somehow (though in an infinite form) be found in God. Thus, faith affirms God as knowing and loving, as relating to us in a personal way.

Other characteristics of faith have already been described when we looked at peak experiences. Again, just briefly, faith is *experienced as gift*. God's gentle attraction, not our own efforts, leads to this relationship. Faith is also *open to challenge*: We cannot prove God's existence, and much in our world (cynicism, violence, tragedy) questions the reality of a good and loving God. Finally, faith is *self-validating*. The experience is its own proof; despite doubts and challenges, we find fulfillment in God.

Summing Up

In the previous chapter we tried to take a serious look at our everyday experiences. We described different types of situations in which people have claimed to experience "something more." With Maslow we have seen that peak experiences are part of full human life. The purpose of this chapter has been to reflect upon those experiences, to search for indications that such experiences can be interpreted as reasonable. With Blondel and Rahner we have seen that such experiences point to the existence of the Infinite and to the structure of the human person as open to the Infinite. With Dulles, we have seen that these experiences can fittingly be called revelation, that God works gently from within to lead us to a deeper appreciation of life and to a closer relationship with God.

Certainly not every warm feeling or good insight is a revelation. But those which give us new light about life's meaning may surely be. Revelation is not lightning bolts or voices or other dramatic events. Revelation is not limited to Moses, Jesus and the disciples. Revelation is the encounter with God which we experience in ourselves, our families and friends, society, the cosmos.

Finally, let's turn again to the banyan tree. At the end of the previous chapter we saw ourselves as new roots, perhaps just budding, perhaps dangling, perhaps reaching into the soil. In this chapter we've been "tilling." Digging into the ground of our experience, we've been looking at our roots and others' roots. And we have drawn upon the work of philosophy and theology to make sure we are well-planted. Although we certainly haven't explored the whole tree (including the main trunk and root), we have found solid and true roots, firmly established in good soil. Our banyan tree is not an illusion, not the product of wishful thinking. We and others can truly encounter God in ordinary life.

For discussion or reflection:

1) Blondel and Rahner both state that a person is a finite being with an infinite capacity. Discuss what this means in terms of your experience.

2) How do specific choices you or people you know have made reflect inner values and vision? How do these choices shape a person?

3) How does Rahner's theory that human knowing points to the existence of the Infinite relate to your experience?

Give examples from your own life or from the lives of people you know.

4) Trace Dulles's steps of discovery through the process of developing a new product: a detergent, a space vehicle or a medication, for instance. Do you think the same process is applicable to religious experience? How would you apply it to whatever beliefs you hold?

CHAPTER THREE

Some Branches:
Appreciating Symbols and Stories

$\mathbf{M}$any people who try to
describe their peak experiences find that language is too limited
to express fully what they have experienced. They search for
the right word or expression, but mere words are not sufficient.
People of all times and cultures have therefore turned to
symbols and stories in their common struggle to describe the
experience of something more.

The Language of Religious Experience

In this chapter, we will look carefully at the means available for
describing our experiences of God. Specifically, we will study
the language of religious experience: signs, symbols, parables
and myths. Then we will see how these pieces fit together and
are used in the Bible. We will also consider the problems related
to this understanding of the Bible as symbolic expression.

In Chapter 1 we tried to get in touch with our own
experiences of something more, and in the next chapter we will
explore just what happened to Moses and Jesus, what can be
said of their experiences of God. But the only way to do this is
through the Scriptures; our only access to Moses and Jesus is
through the writings of the communities that resulted from
their lives. So our investigation of signs, symbols, parables and
myths in this chapter will help us understand the Scriptures
and enter into the experiences of Moses and Jesus. Symbols and

stories are the branches which nourish us (the new roots) and connect us ultimately to Jesus—the trunk of our Christian banyan tree.

This study of the Scriptures also anticipates our look at organized religion. Since all things cannot be said or studied simultaneously, we will postpone a careful look at the community, the communal nature of religious experience and the place of Scriptures until Chapter 5. For now, we will concentrate on sign, symbol, parable and myth as important tools for communicating experiences of God and for studying the lives of Moses and Jesus.

Sign and Symbol

We start with signs. Simple and direct, they are found in both secular and religious life. Signs stand for or point to a specific person or object or event. But there is no intrinsic relationship between the sign and its object; the connection must be *learned*.

Signs have meaning because people agree that this sign will have this meaning. For example, society has agreed that a red light means stop. There is no intrinsic connection between red and stop, but we have learned that meaning and agree to it (more or less!).

Language provides another example: The word *tree* is associated with a particular physical object. Those of us who speak English relate the word (in print or in sound) to the real object. Someone just learning English must learn this connection. One characteristic of signs is very evident in this examples: Signs are not ambiguous; they clearly represent one thing. In religion, too, there are many signs which recall a historical event and its significance for faith. Think of a Catholic church, where stained-glass windows, banners, and statues signify the Catholic heritage. For example, the crib scene recalls the whole Christmas story.

Another characteristic of signs is that they work simply at the level of object-knowledge. Signs merely designate something for our convenience, but they do not open up new areas of knowledge or experience. They merely point to what is already known or believed. Signs do not get "inside" that which they signify; nor do they engage our own subjectivity.

A third characteristic of signs is that they are limited to a particular group—the group which determines the meaning of the sign or at least agrees to its continued use. For example, white is a sign of purity in the West, but in the East it is a sign of death, the color of mourning. Some signs, as in mathematics and science, have become almost universal, but even this is due to mutual agreement.

A sign can acquire a deeper level of meaning if it becomes associated with a particular experience or set of experiences. Take, for example, the flag. That piece of cloth of arbitrary colors and design can evoke great and differing reactions: pride and loyalty, respect and obedience, fear and hatred. Think of the powerful images associated with it: an American astronaut saluting the flag on the moon, an angry mob burning it in violent protest. A sign with this much evocative power begins to approach what we mean by a symbol.

Probably the best example in Christianity of a sign charged with symbolic power is the cross (indeed, we speak of the *"Sign* of the Cross"). The cross has the primary characteristic of a sign: It is not ambiguous; it clearly identifies a person, an object, a building as Christian.

Yet the choice of the cross was not arbitrary. It represented a key event in the life and mission of Jesus. To many the choice was controversial; to many simply absurd. For the cross in the Roman empire was an instrument of pain and torture, a sign of tyranny.

But for the early Christian community the cross was transformed by Jesus' resurrection; the cross pointed beyond death to victory over death.

Interestingly, the cross has emphasized different realities at different times in the Christian era. The focus was first on Christ's triumph over death, but later switched to Jesus' suffering on the cross. At times the cross became identified with oppressive political power; at still other times, it was a sign of hope of liberation.

In all these examples, the cross is a sign, yet it possesses the power of a symbol. The cross has such power because it is associated with true symbols: the shedding of blood, resurrection, kingship. When, then, is the difference between a sign and a symbol?

In ordinary conversation we often equate sign and symbol, but there is a very real difference. Symbols are not determined by social agreement (the traffic light); they are not made by our creative imagination (the flag). Symbols arise out of life; their existence is a given and they allow us to get in touch with a deeper meaning and reality.

Darkness and water and the sun are common symbols. Simply a given part of life on this planet, these realities come to be invested with a deeper meaning; for example, the sun has become a symbol of creative power. When we confront such a symbol, our unconscious self connects with this deeper meaning. (The unconscious self here means a latent awareness, a knowledge we don't know we have until the insight occurs.) Symbols are not determined by arbitrary decision. And the most powerful symbols are universal.

At the same time, symbols have great versatility. Unlike a sign, which refers specifically to one object, a symbol may speak of many things. For example, water is ambivalent in its symbolic meaning. It suggests nurture and new life, refreshment (think about what water means to a desert people); but water also suggests danger and threat to life (think about the destruction a flood wreaks). Such ambivalence is due in part to differences in culture, geography and the experience of nature. Thus a symbol may be used in a variety of ways and may evoke new and different insights.

Symbols are not infinitely flexible, however. A symbol has power because it *participates in the reality it symbolizes*. This relationship to the deeper reality is limited by the symbol itself, for a symbol can reveal only what is present within it. Water is a versatile symbol, but the physical properties of water and its uses at the same time limit this versatility. Water cannot symbolize warmth and light—the properties of fire. A symbol can only convey a meaning that is somehow related to the qualities of the symbol.

Symbols have greater power than signs. Unlike signs, which are limited to objective, observable aspects of human experience, symbols attempt to get to the *subjective*—felt, experienced—level of meaning and value. Symbols attempt to grasp what is not immediately known, to deepen knowledge, to express the meaning of existence. Symbols have power because through these aspects of the visible world (water, darkness, fire, etc.) we catch a glimpse of something more; we appreciate a deeper dimension of life.

Symbols give us a way to talk about the infinite reality we explored with the help of Maslow, Blondel, Rahner and Dulles. Symbols are tools we use, elements we borrow from the physical world, to point to the Infinite.

As we saw in Chapter 1, our experiences of God occur in and through our experiences of ourselves, family and friends, society, the cosmos. The power of symbols helps us to recognize and express this deeper dimension of our day-to-day existence. Without symbols, this depth could be missed and our sense of life flattened out.

So far all our examples of symbols have been taken from nature. There are also personal symbols—mother, father, teacher, one who loves—which better express person-to-person relationships. This, of course, is most significant when we use symbols to describe our relationship with God. The emphasis falls on intersubjectivity, on personal encounter.

Unlike signs, symbols always allow us to experience emotionally charged meaning. The person as subject gets involved. Symbols involve much more than the intellectual knowledge or the logical assent to a proposition demanded by signs. Symbols evoke the kind of experience in which the *whole* person—head and heart—responds. Symbols allow us to get in touch with and take a stance toward the basic questions of life.

But how do we know if symbols are true and correct? Only from our experience and our history. If the symbol "works" for us—that is, if it promotes this relationship with something more—then we can recognize the symbol's truth. As with peak experiences, however, there is the possibility of illusion. Symbols can be abused, even become idols. So historical indications are also important. If the symbol is used over long periods of time, then it seems to be a satisfactory symbol. If it continues to ring true in people's experiences, to improve the human condition, and to create healthy existence, then the symbol is validated.

By way of summary, we can state six characteristics of symbols: (1) Symbols, like signs, point beyond themselves to something other. (2) Symbols, unlike signs, participate in the reality they describe. (3) Symbols give us knowledge of ultimate reality which cannot be obtained in other ways. (4) Symbols unlock dimensions of our spirit which correspond to reality. (5) Symbols are not created solely by acts of the conscious will, but must be assented to by the unconscious. (6) Symbols can grow and change and even lose their significance.

Pause and reflect on your own experience. What symbols speak to you of "something more"?

Parable

A third form of symbolic language is the parable—the narrative form of symbolism used by Jesus.

Parables are very similar to symbols in their purpose and power. But they are not physical elements like fire or darkness or personal relationships like mother or lover; they are stories. Like symbols, parables grow out of human experience: They allow us to get in touch with some deeper meaning by comparison with some ordinary situation in life. Jesus taught about the Reign of God by using parables about planting seeds, losing a sheep, family arguments and other ordinary events. Because such events were familiar to all, part of common knowledge, Jesus could be sure these stories (and their deeper meaning) would be directly understood and accepted by the people.

The purpose of the parable, then, is to make one point, the heart of the story. The purpose is not a one-to-one correspondence between every detail of the parable and a series of applications (that's an allegory). The hearers of Jesus' parables either got the moral of the story or simply missed it.

Because parables are closely linked with everyday life, later hearers may have difficulty with changing cultural circumstances. Some of Jesus' parables depend on an understanding of the customs and situations of his day. We probably miss the point of the parable if, for example, we have no idea that three measures of flour equal enough for 50 pounds of bread (see Luke 13:20-21). We need some knowledge of the customs, politics and social setting of Jesus' time in order to appreciate the parable fully.

Still, the meaning of a parable is not limited to a particular place and time. Given some understanding of the cultural circumstances, parables (like symbols) can be used in many situations. The meaning of a parable can be applied again and again in different times and places, because this deeper meaning (like the meaning symbols convey) is rooted in the very nature of human life. The everyday details in Jesus' parables may no longer be part of our culture (leprosy, sheep, particular farming techniques), but the realities of healing, trust and faith are. In a parable we can still see ourselves; we can still be enlightened and challenged by its meaning.

Parables, like symbols, help us to appreciate deeper dimensions of reality, to come to new insights. Parables help us to see ourselves as we really are, and they also open up knowledge of something more. That is why Jesus used parables to try to communicate his understanding of the Reign of God, to lead people into a new relationship with Abba. (We will see more of this in the next chapter.)

But parables lead to more than just understanding; they lead to a decision. The hearers of Jesus' parables were confronted with a choice: commitment or rejection. The Gospels tell us that both choices were made by those who listened to Jesus.

Parables, again like symbols, are validated in our experience. They cannot be judged by debate rules or other such criteria. Parables appeal to our imagination and to our intuitive knowledge. We accept the parable because we see ourselves in it and find truth.

Myth

A fourth form of religious language is myth. This topic needs very special attention both because of frequent misunderstanding of the term and because of myth's significance. In ordinary usage, *myth* refers to a falsehood or a fairy tale or a commonly held but incorrect story: "Myths of motherhood shattered"; "Dispelling grim mid-life myths." This ordinary meaning of myth is too limited. We must learn a new—and correct—definition of myth, one which points to myth's richness and truth. Therefore please note: *Myth* is a good word; it speaks of truth!

How did *myth* come to be understood as "not true"? Several factors seem to be involved. Early study of myth was largely limited to Greek and Roman literature. But by the classical period of Greece and Rome, the faith which first led to the formation of the myths had been lost, and they had become mere fiction. People had difficulty believing in the gods of the myths. So the focus on Greek and Roman myths led to the conclusion that myths were simply imaginative stories.

A second factor was the development of the scientific mentality and worldview. The modern Western world viewed progress as the key for interpreting history. As a result, the ancient world with its myths was judged naive and childish. Similarly, myths were often judged in comparison with scientific ideas. Thus myths were classified according to the scientific questions they seemed to be answering, for example, creation and the working of the cosmos.

The metaphorical nature of myths was missed. Myths do not say explicitly that one thing is *like* another; they speak directly. For example, "God created the world in six days" is myth; it should not be read as either science or history. Such myth has been criticized for inventing gods in order to provide solutions to questions in nature which could not be otherwise explained. But this oversimplified scientific approach fails to see that myths do not attempt to answer scientific questions but questions of meaning and value. The first chapters of Genesis do not attempt to give a scientific account about creation but do proclaim a faith in the Creator God. (Later in this chapter we will study this example in more detail.)

The third factor which led to the misunderstanding of myth was the loss of a religious worldview. Appreciating a myth demands a certain kind of faith. Recall Dulles' statement in the last chapter: Insight comes to those who both puzzle over reality and have a confidence that the problem can be solved (see p. 35). Myth presupposes certain stance toward the question. Myths cannot speak to those who shut themselves off from faith. In fact, some of the criticism of myth may well have come from the desire to discredit faith and religion.

Fortunately, we now have a renewed understanding and appreciation of myth. Other ancient societies have been investigated in which myths were experienced as alive and positive. These myths were at the heart of a culture and worldview—what gave meaning and direction to people's lives. Other research has shown how mythological ideas seem rooted in human nature and are found in many different peoples, allowing them to express fundamental hopes and fears about life. Thus myth has been recognized as a distinctive form of expression. Rather than a sign of naivete and backwardness in prescientific cultures, anthropologists and theologians now appreciate myth as rich in intelligence and insight. Indeed, myth offers a unique means of communication—a means lost to the scientific mentality—a means of expressing the experience of revelation.

How, then, is myth to be understood? We can begin by relating myth to what we have already studied: symbol and parable. Indeed, a myth can be understood as a *symbolic story*. Myths possess the qualities of symbol rather than sign. That is, myths are not simply determined by social agreement; they arise out of life. Like parables myths view reality directly, making no distinction between symbol and that which is symbolized. The meaning of the myth is perceived directly through the story.

Myths are rich in meaning, providing access to fundamental dimensions of life. Myths also have great versatility; they speak of many things and can be retold at many moments in life. Thus a myth related to birth can also be applied to other significant passages: adulthood, marriage, death.

Myths have profound power. They do not merely point to some object, but provide a bridge to deeper meaning. They evoke from people a total response, a sense of commitment;

myths touch people in a personal, subjective way. While the language of the myth is related to a particular time, place and culture, the meaning of the myth is more universal, for it is concerned with the most significant aspects of human existence. No author is ever given, therefore, because myths emerge from common human life and express universal themes.

Like parables, myths may not be understood by later generations because of unfamiliarity with the particular situation. But once the situation becomes familiar, all the audiences need is spiritual perceptivity. Compared to parables, myths are much more complex. Parables attempt to make one point, while myths speak to all of life and even provide a total view of life itself—that is, a framework in which all of life can be understood and interpreted.

Myths have other unique features. First, some gods are always involved in these symbolic stories. As a result, if the myth is to be understood and appreciated, the nature and role of the gods must be discovered. The key for this understanding is the realization that the mythological attitude sees everything in the world as possessing personal life: trees, rivers, storms, and so on. Some scholars note an underlying unity beneath the stories of these many gods. They point to the variety of gods as simply a reflection of human perception which experiences the divine in a variety of ways. (Of course a major breakthrough in Judaism, continued in Christianity, was the belief in only one God. Accordingly, Judeo-Christian myths speak of this one God.)

Another characteristic of myth is its use of symbolic space and time. Distance is used as a symbol of separation, of a breakdown in the relationship between the divine and humans. Recall how Adam and Eve were sent out of the garden, no longer able to walk with God. The use of time is also symbolic. Myths are not some kind of scientific explanation for the beginnings of the cosmos; they do not look back to a particular time. Rather, myths describe stories which can help people interpret the events which happen in their lives. Thus the events which took place "in the beginning" also indicate how things are to be today. The gods teach human beings the meaning of their lives.

Myths are clearly very significant for the human community. They provide a unique means of speaking the truth—the truth about the major events of life, about the meaning of existence, about relationship with God. Myths allow finite human beings to meet and express the Infinite.

Myth in Scripture

To help us appreciate the meaning and function of myths, let's look at the opening chapters of Genesis. Perhaps the first item to note is that Genesis presents *two* different accounts of creation. In the first chapter. God creates the world and everything in it during six days of work and rests on the seventh day. Genesis describes God's creation of human beings on the sixth day in this way: "God created man in his image;/in the divine image he created him;/male and female he created them" (1:27).

The second chapter presents a very different story. Here there are no days, but there are more concrete details: God plants a garden in Eden, rivers are named. Then the human being is created—before beasts and birds. This second story of human creation goes this way: "The LORD God formed man out of the clay of the ground and blew into his nostrils the breath of life, and so man became a living being" (2:7). Only later, after no "suitable partner" had been found, is woman created. "So the LORD God cast a deep sleep on the man, and while he was asleep, he took out one of his ribs and closed up its place with flesh. The LORD God then built up into a woman the rib that he had taken from the man" (2:21-22).

Two creation stories? Which one is true? We may be tempted to ask that question, but it is the *wrong* question. This question reflects our scientific mentality asking Genesis to do something it never intended: give scientific facts (how creation happened). If instead we accept Genesis as myth, we can approach the stories in a different way. Both are true! Both convey fundamental truths: God is the source of all life; we are dependent on God; we are precious for we are created in God's image.

Let's not rush past this point. The very fact that there are two creation accounts should wave a red flag about proper interpretation of Genesis. The correct question to ask of Genesis is, "What does it mean?" To force Genesis into categories of either history (as we know history) or science is to do violence to Scripture. The Genesis stories speak of ultimate values, of the meaning of existence, of relationship with God. There is no attempt (even though Genesis has often been interpreted this way) to present scientific fact. Developments in science—the theory of evolution, for example—neither disprove Genesis nor deny God's creative power. The theory of evolution and the Book of Genesis represent two entirely different perspectives.

Many religions have some kind of creation myth. This should not be surprising, for living life raises such questions as, "Where did we come from?" and, "What's life all about?" Peoples of many different times and places have tried to answer these questions in their myths. Creation stories often have common elements. Water almost always appears in the very beginning. (Water, as we have already seen, is a most appropriate symbol for it suggests danger and destruction as well as nourishment and life.) And from water emerges land, the prerequisite for life. Notice how these two elements are found in Genesis.

Other myths often go on to describe the emergence of the gods at this point, and then a battle between good and evil. Genesis differs by expressing Judaism's belief that one God is the source of all life. The struggle with evil enters only after the couple sins.

In the third chapter of Genesis, the story continues. Sin enters creation—not from God, but from the human beings. Genesis describes a conversation between a serpent and the woman, and then states, "The woman saw that the tree was good for food, pleasing to the eyes, and desirable for gaining wisdom. So she took some of its fruit and ate it; and she also gave some to her husband, who was with her, and he ate it" (3:6). Sin and evil enter the world through the free choice of the two humans, not from a good God. The woman is punished by pain in childbirth, the man by hard work to get food. The couple is then expelled from the garden.

Physical evil and personal evil (sin) are realities which have always confronted the human family. We ask, "Why?" We search for some explanation for so much suffering. Recall our description of the experience of tragedy as a source either of despair or of hope (see pp. 19-20). Evil truly is an ambiguous reality; it is also inescapable. The Bible devotes an entire book (Job) to pondering this issue. And the recent book *Why Do Bad Things Happen to Good People* was a best-seller in the United States. Thousands of years pass, but we still grapple with the problem of evil. It makes sense, then, that this problem was included in our fundamental myth, in the very opening chapters of the Bible.

The Genesis story goes on, describing the growth of the human family: the birth of Cain, Abel and many other sons and daughters. But as the number grew, so did the evil. First Cain kills Abel. Then the wickedness is so great that God says, "I will wipe out from the earth the men whom I have created, and not only the men, but also the beasts and the creeping things and the birds of the air, for I am sorry that I made them" (6:7)—except for Noah, who is spared from the flood and becomes a second beginning of the human family. Genesis describes how God blessed Noah and his children, saying, "Be fertile and multiply and fill the earth" (9:1b). Once again the human family grew. And once again the problem of evil surfaced, as symbolized in the story of the Tower of Babel (11:1-9).

The first 11 chapters of Genesis, then, serve as a prologue to the stories of the patriarchs (Abraham, Isaac, Jacob, Joseph), the exodus from Egypt and the covenant at Sinai. For the people of Israel, God's intervention in history, especially in saving and choosing this people, represented the center of their belief. The prehistory—the myths in Genesis—must be read in this light, for this prehistory sets the stage for these later events. The opening chapters of Genesis were written for a religious purpose: to stress God's plan and initiative in history. Thus the setting is prepared for God's special intervention in his call to Abraham in Genesis 12.

Modern scholars have greatly helped us understand the opening chapters of Genesis. Although we cannot absolutely rule out the possibility of a direct revelation which describes all the events of creation, is it not very likely. God's action in history does not seem to take place in this way. Besides, careful analysis of the text shows that there probably was a natural and complex beginning and development of the story. For example, these 11 chapters are the work of several authors who used materials closely related to other sources, such as stories from Mesopotamia. Israel's experience of God cried out for expression. So the Hebrews borrowed from these other myths but transformed them in telling about their unique religious experience. Israel's theological perspective (belief in one God) radically changed the popular Mesopotamian framework and imagery and gave it new meaning.

It is so very important, then, to appreciate Genesis as myth. If we look for science or history, we will miss the true meaning of the stories. Only through myth can we fully enter into relationship and accept the God of Israel as the God of all nature and of all history. Only through myth can we fully appreciate our own dignity as God's creatures and our own alienation from God and from one another. Only through myth can we fully experience salvation history.

Pause and reflect on your own experience. What stories have led you to deeper insight? Would you call them parables or myths?

Obstacles to Understanding

If myth is so important then why do many of us have difficulty understanding and accepting myth? There are two very common, yet very different, reasons: our scientific mentality and the literal reading of the Bible. Each is widespread; each significantly hinders a proper appreciation of Scripture. Therefore, it is necessary for us to take a careful look at these two influences in our lives.

The Scientific Worldview

The computer certainly is not the cause of the scientific mentality, only its latest expression. For hundreds of years humans have been viewing their world and themselves in a more and more objective way. At the time of the Reformation, the symbolic approach to life was already under challenge. In religion, symbols had been reduced to signs, even to magic. The reaction was to strip away not only the abuses but the symbols, too. Protestant theologians seemed to create greater distance between God and sinful human beings; the things of earth could no longer be trusted to reveal the divine.

The movement toward objectivity led to viewing the world as a machine. First God was placed outside the machine, necessary only to keep it going and then to fill in any gaps in understanding. As science developed and people understood more and more, however, God became unnecessary. The model of the machine was applied first to astronomy and physics, then to biology, sociology and psychology. Such a mechanistic worldview clearly has no room for symbol and myth. God is eliminated, and so is *personal* involvement with others and the world. The human ends up being compared to a computer.

Although the mechanistic model is now rejected in theory, its symbolic power remains; many people still look at the universe as something to be used and manipulated. The sense of the sacred has been lost; it is very difficult to find an appropriate symbol for expressing the divine. The result, of course, is disastrous. People attempt to hang on to the Scriptures even while accepting the scientific worldview. They combine Scripture and science, for example, and try to harmonize evolution with Genesis.

Since we are people of our time, it should not surprise us that we find these tendencies within ourselves. The scientific mentality is probably our mentality. Perhaps we try to harmonize science and symbol. Or perhaps we find little meaning in symbols and turn away. Or perhaps we try to impose some intellectual meaning instead of letting the meaning emerge from the reality. It probably is not an exaggeration to describe our time as a time of crisis. It is very difficult for many of us to appreciate the richness of symbol and myth. Yet that is the language with which faith is remembered and expressed and handed on.

Biblical Literalism

The second major hindrance in understanding and accepting myth is the literal reading of the Bible. This fundamentalism is very different from the scientific mentality and yet, curiously, very similar to it.

Take the Genesis story, for example. The fundamentalist will hold that the story is factually true and that there is no room for evolution. Yet the mental attitude is remarkably similar to the scientific mentality, treating the Scriptures as scientific and historical texts. It is very fact-oriented, approaching everything as an object.

In the present situation in the United States, the worldview of biblical literalism must be taken very seriously. It appears not only in school-board hearings, court cases, fundamentalist Churches, evangelical television programs and politics, but also throughout our culture. The literalist perspective challenges most of us; thinking and expressing ourselves symbolically is becoming a lost art.

This mentality has a certain appeal: It offers a certain simplicity, conviction and power. Perhaps at the heart of its appeal is the offer of security. In a very complex world, it gives neat and simple answers. This is also its greatest liability, for it offers a false security, maintained only by a rigid dogmatism. Biblical literalism strips away the rich meanings of symbol and myth and replaces them with words which are allowed to mean only one thing. That is a terrible price to pay for a false security.

Thus the great problem with biblical literalism is the flattening out of the symbolic depth of the texts. Instead of fostering the symbolic imagination, the fundamentalist spends more and more energy ingeniously defending the mentality. What is more important is not faith in the divine, but belief in a particular theory of Scripture.

For an example, let's return to the creation story in Genesis. The literalist debate over the facts of creation misses the meaning of Genesis. As we have already seen, Genesis is similar to other creation stories; one major difference is the monotheism of the Jewish faith. This belief in one God is central to Genesis. As the people of Israel told and wrote and heard the story of creation, they were reminded of this fundamental belief. A key issue in Genesis is the description of the people's experience of God as one, that is, the affirmation of monotheism against polytheism and all the other foreign beliefs which tempted the people of Israel. Not only did Israel experience God as one, but also it experienced all the elements of earth as God's creatures, not gods in themselves (as did other religions). Because of the pressure and influences of these other religions, faith was hard, idolatry easy. But questions about science or history would never have entered Hebrew minds.

Biblical literalism must be seen for what it is: an approach to Scripture which provides easy answers but shallow religion. The depth of experience—both in Scripture and in today's world—is easily missed. The fundamentalism which grows out of this biblical literalism strips Christianity of its history, tradition and symbolic expressions; it offers a false security while removing Christianity's relevance for tasks in our world today. The literalist mentality is "either-or"; absolute, barren. It fails to appreciate the richness and depth and variety of symbols and myths—of human life.

Yet the literalist mentality does exist in many of us, even if not in a complete, fundamentalist way. We have been taught that the Bible is God's word. We have heard various interpretations of Scripture, but we react to these interpretations in different ways. Some find much life through contemporary scholarship; others find confusion and perhaps turn spontaneously to a more literalist perspective.

In the next two chapters we will see in more detail how the Bible is God's word. We will also use the insights of this chapter to appreciate that word, to enter into the richness and meaning of symbol and myth.

Pause and reflect on your own experience. What difficulties have you encountered in Scripture? What insights have you found?

Summing Up

One more time: Myths are good! They are symbolic expressions of an intuitive grasp of reality. Myths engage the whole person, provoking attitudes and evoking feelings. Myths address questions of ultimate concern and speak of truth.

Myths form some of the major branches on our banyan tree. Let's return to our imaginary consideration of its maze of roots and branches. We are those new roots—just budding or dangling or sinking into the soil. These new roots are attached to solid branches, and some of the most important of these branches are myths. These symbolic stories not only preserve the most significant realities of faith and life but also allow us to enter into them. For example, the Genesis myth leads us to an encounter with the Creator God and to an appreciation of the dignity of every human being, for each person is created in God's image. (We will consider in detail other examples in the next chapter.) Myths, along with symbols and parables, provide a unique means of communication, a way for finite beings to express and experience the Infinite. In a word, myths are necessary for connecting us to the original trunk of our banyan tree, Jesus.

For discussion or reflection:

1) Signs and symbols are often confused. Reflect on the differences between them, giving examples from your own life.

2) What symbols help you grasp deeper meanings with your whole self—heart and head? Why do symbols do this better than rational thought?

3) What is your favorite parable? What truth does it express to you?

4) What is your understanding of the word myth? *What myths help you grasp the meaning of life?*

5) What traces of the scientific mentality and biblical literalism do you have to struggle against in your own life?

6) How do you attempt to find meaning in Scripture?

CHAPTER FOUR

Old Roots:
Focusing on Moses and Jesus

In Chapter 1 we reflected on our everyday lives—on ourselves, the people in our lives, society, the cosmos. We also listened to some claims (and perhaps agreed with them) that there is "something more"— that God can be experienced in and through the events of life, in nature and love, tragedy and religion. Then we stepped back from our experience to ask how this is possible and to search for means of communicating such an experience. We discovered that the experience of revelation can be an authentic human experience and that we need symbols and myths to describe our encounters with God.

In this chapter, then, we will build on all these insights as we investigate the lives of Moses and Jesus. Specifically, we want to ask them, "What happened in your life? What was your experience of God?" The only way to answer these questions is to listen to the Scriptures, to hear what Jewish and Christian communities have told us about Moses and Jesus.

Why do we want to investigate the experiences of Moses and Jesus? First, they serve as examples of persons who have experienced something more. Since Moses and Jesus were human beings, their lives will help us appreciate more deeply the experience of revelation. We can expect to find basic similarities between their historical experiences and contemporary experiences of revelation. Second, their experiences have become the foundations of two world religions. Clearly their lives call for particular attention.

Moses and Jesus therefore demonstrate the two main topics of this book—human experience and religious tradition. Indeed, the life of Jesus is the trunk of our Christian banyan tree. But we can understand Jesus only if we appreciate his roots in Judaism.

Although Judaism claims Abraham as its "father in faith," it was Moses who molded Abraham's descendants as well as other peoples into the nation of Israel during the exodus. In fact, the experience described in the Book of Exodus is the experience not only of Moses but also of the whole people. So let's turn, then, to the experience of Moses and the Hebrew people.

The Experience of Moses and the Hebrews

To enter into this experience, let's turn to the story of Moses as told in the biblical Book of Exodus. After recalling the history of Abraham's descendants in Egypt and their increasing oppression by the pharaohs, Exodus describes the birth of Moses (2:1-10). Careful details explain how the infant Moses was saved from the pharaoh's command that all baby boys be killed and how he was raised by the pharaoh's daughter. It is a colorful story, not unlike stories other cultures tell of the births of great leaders.

Our discussion of myth reminds us not to ask, "Did it really happen this way?" but instead, "What is the meaning of this story?" The story clearly states that Moses is someone special; even from birth he is favored by God.

Exodus then jumps ahead to picture Moses as a man who, despite his privileged status in the pharaoh's court, remembers and defends his own people. He kills an Egyptian who has attacked a Hebrew. When the event becomes known, Moses flees Egypt and settles among a kindred Semitic people in Sinai (Exodus 2:11-22). This brief history sets the stage for Moses' call.

The familiar story in Exodus 3:1—4:17 is rich in colorful details. While caring for his sheep, Moses comes upon a bush, which is burning yet is not being consumed by the fire. From the bush a voice addresses Moses, identifying the speaker as the God of Abraham, Isaac and Jacob. This God expresses concern for the Hebrews and promises to save them through the leadership of Moses. Moses responds with a long list of questions and doubts and excuses, basically saying to God, "Don't you want to pick somebody else?" God answers Moses each time, first promising to be with him, then revealing the divine name as "I am who am," then giving instructions, then working wonders to convince Moses (turning his staff into a serpent) and, finally, sending Aaron to speak for Moses.

This wonderful dialogue is a *symbolic account* of a profound human experience—vocation. The pattern will be repeated again and again in the Bible, especially in the writings of the prophets: God calls; the person responds, often with hesitation; God comforts the person and tells the individual to fear not; finally, God commissions the person to speak God's word. But what does it all mean? Surely the Hebrews wanted to proclaim the special character of Moses, both as their leader and as a symbol of the people's own experience of being chosen. And so this section describes God's call to Moses.

Was there really a burning bush? By now we should know that this is the wrong question! The story was not written to give this kind of information. It was written to describe God's action in the life of Moses and the Hebrew people.

Let's retell the story, using ordinary language: Moses was a Hebrew who had fled Egypt after getting into some trouble. He settled with some friendly people, married, had children and became a shepherd. All in all his life was quite pleasant, especially in comparison with the oppressed life other Hebrews lived in Egypt. Shepherding allowed Moses lots of quiet time. He found himself thinking about his people in Egypt and how they were suffering. He prayed. Gradually he recognized that living a comfortable life was not for him; more and more he sensed a responsibility, a need to get involved. He sensed that God was calling him to action in the events of his life and his people's. He decided to return to Egypt, to risk all to be faithful to his vocation.

This account conveys the same meaning as the biblical account, but it certainly does not engage us in the same way

Exodus does. Burning bushes and conversations with God grab our attention and get us involved in the deeper reality and meaning. That, of course, is the purpose of such stories. The historical event may actually have been closer to our ordinary account, but the *reality* of the experience is better communicated by the creative story.

In our own day we hear the stories of contemporary religious leaders such as Mother Teresa and Martin Luther King, Jr. It should not be surprising that their experiences contain the same basic elements as Moses': sensitivity, courage, faith in discerning and responding to God's call. But we also tell our stories, our history, in very different ways and we cannot force Exodus into our pattern. The Bible uses symbolic stories to speak of truth, in this case, God's call of Moses.

It is also important to remember that hundreds of years passed between the historical exodus event and its symbolic description in writing. The exodus occurred around 1280 B.C. But the oldest written sources of the first five books of the Bible, the Pentateuch, date from the ninth century B.C. And the Pentateuch as we now have it was not composed until the fifth century B.C.

The Exodus

Let's now turn to the account of the exodus story (Exodus 12:1—14:31).

Exodus 12 begins rather curiously with Moses giving directions on how to celebrate the Passover feast. Many details about food and its preparation are stated, for example, the meat is to be roasted and eaten with unleavened bread and bitter herbs. This carefully planned festival is celebrating an event which, as the story is told in the text, has not yet happened! So what is going on here?

This is where the dates help. After leaving Egypt around 1280 B.C. and wandering in the desert, the Hebrew people settled in the land of Canaan, the Promised Land, where they eventually flourished. At times of special celebration, they remembered the most sacred time of their history (the exodus and Sinai covenant). So rituals developed, combining these particular celebrations with the exodus story. For example,

Passover was an ancient feast antedating the exodus itself. It was a rite seminomadic peoples celebrated in the spring to ensure the fecundity of the flock and to ward off evil and hostile powers (Exodus 12:1-14, 21-28). The agricultural feast of Unleavened Bread was celebrated to give thanks for the barley harvest (Exodus 12:15-20; 13:3-10). Over the centuries, the celebration of these feasts was connected with the exodus experience. When the first books of the Bible were finally composed, the writers tended to depict the detailed laws and festivals of the Israelite kingdom (their current experience) as originating within the context of the historic escape from Egypt.

This combination of later liturgical development (the celebration of the feasts) with the original experience is a common way for remembering and handing on such experience (as we'll see in Chapter 5). Placing the details of this celebration directly into the text itself (having Moses give specific details of the menu!) emphasizes the significance of the ritual. Thus Moses says:

"You shall observe this as a perpetual ordinance for yourselves and your descendants. Thus, you must also observe this rite when you have entered the land which the LORD will give you as he promised. When your children ask you, 'What does this rite of yours mean?' you shall reply, 'This is the Passover sacrifice of the LORD, who passed over the houses of the Israelites in Egypt; when he struck down the Egyptians, he spared our houses.'"

(Exodus 12:24-27).

In Exodus 12—14, then, we find descriptions of later liturgical celebrations intertwined with stories of the original event. (We must remember, of course, that these stories themselves are already symbolic in form.) After talking of menus and liturgical rules, Exodus finally describes the departure of the Israelites from Egypt.

This story too is a familiar one: the Hebrews being led by God, described as a pillar of cloud and a pillar of fire; the Egyptians chasing after the Hebrews; the parting of the sea with the Hebrews escaping and the Egyptians being destroyed. Again the symbols are rich: God is expressed as fire and water—both of which are life-giving and destructive. Such a story allows future generations of Jews (and, much later, us) also to enter into this sacred experience—the experience of being saved by God. For it was Yahweh who led the Hebrews safely from Egypt.

Exodus is very clear about this point: God is the true savior and liberator; Moses is simply God's assistant. And so we read such lines as these: "...[God] rerouted them toward the Red Sea by way of the desert road" (13:18); "The LORD himself will fight for you..." (14:14); "...The LORD swept the sea with a strong east wind throughout the night and so turned it into dry land" (14:21); "The Egyptians were fleeing head on toward the sea, when the LORD hurled them into its midst" (14:27); "When Israel saw the Egyptians lying dead on the seashore and beheld the great power that the LORD had shown against the Egyptians, they feared the LORD and believed in him and in his servant Moses" (14:30-31).

Did the sea really part? Once again, that's the wrong question! The historical fact that lies behind the Exodus story is this: The Hebrews were oppressed and they escaped to freedom. Some of the details of that escape may be embellishments of natural events. But the purpose of the Hebrew Scriptures is to tell of a fundamental experience of God's action in the life of the people.

If the whole event could somehow have been recorded on videotape, what would we see? We must admit that we cannot say with certitude. But if we take seriously what earlier chapters have said about the experience of revelation—that God is encountered in and through ordinary events—then it is likely that the same ordinary events were present in the Exodus. Just as God can be experienced in and through nature or love or tragedy, so God could be encountered in the flight from oppression.

What then might we see on our videotape? Probably a refugee people fleeing before a powerful army, a group often discouraged and lost and yet having hope, a people who kept faith and talked of finding God in the midst of it all. In our own day, we do see such refugees on TV; we do hear oppressed people speak of their trust that God is delivering them to freedom. This is the story of the Hebrews and of Yahweh who led them to freedom.

The Covenant

This deliverance in the exodus event is the first half of Judaism's foundational experience; the second is the Covenant.

As the Book of Exodus continues its story, God's choice of Moses and the people is ratified in a solemn agreement. After presenting some of the trials a refugee people faces in the desert (lack of food and water, battles with foreign peoples) and evidence of God's care for them, Exodus describes the sacred experience at Mount Sinai (19:1—24:18). First God and Moses have a conversation in which God's intention is announced: "You have seen for yourselves how I treated the Egyptians and how I bore you up on eagle wings and brought you here to myself. Therefore, if you hearken to my voice and keep my covenant, you shall be my special possession, dearer to me than all other people, though all the earth is mine" (Exodus 19:4b-5).

After several more conversations, Moses finally gathers the people. The encounter is marvelously described:

> On the morning of the third day there were peals of thunder and lightning, and a heavy cloud over the mountain, and a very loud trumpet blast, so that all the people in the camp trembled. But Moses led the people out of the camp to meet God, and they stationed themselves at the foot of the mountain. Mount Sinai was all wrapped in smoke, for the LORD came down upon it in fire. The smoke rose from it as though from a furnace, and the whole mountain trembled violently. The trumpet blast grew louder and louder, while Moses was speaking and God answering him with thunder.
>
> When the LORD came down to the top of Mount Sinai, he summoned Moses to the top of the mountain, and Moses went up to him.
>
> (Exodus 19:16-20)

In this solemn context Moses receives the Ten Commandments (Exodus 20:1-17) and many other laws and regulations (Exodus 20:22—23:33). After Moses has explained all these to the people, they respond, "We will do everything that the LORD has told us" (Exodus 24:3b).

The covenant between God and the Hebrews is then ratified in a ritual. Moses has an altar built and young bulls sacrificed. He pours half their blood on the altar. Then, after reading some of God's decrees, Moses "took the blood and sprinkled it on the people, saying, 'This is the blood of the covenant which the LORD has made with you in accordance with all these words of his'" (Exodus 24:8).

Covenant—this word captures the very heart of the Jewish experience. This people has been chosen as God's very own, and they have responded with complete commitment. God will be their God and will continue to protect them; the people will show their commitment by keeping God's law.

In the symbolic ratification of this covenant, Moses pours blood on the altar and sprinkles it on the people. For the Jews blood was a symbol for the very life of a living being. By sprinkling blood on the altar (which represents God) and on the people, Moses symbolically expresses the conviction that the covenant partners (God and the people) share a common life.

The Jewish people articulate their experience of God, especially how God had chosen them, in a variety of ways—father-son, marriage, shepherd and flock. Yet the key idea for expressing this relationship between God and Israel is "covenant."

In the second millennium B.C. a covenant was a common type of political treaty, a verbal agreement between a more powerful party and a less powerful one. Technically this type of pact was called a suzerainty treaty. Thus Israel borrowed an already existing political image in its attempt to express its relationship with God.

In such a treaty the more powerful party makes certain promises, even though the more powerful party is not strictly obliged to keep them. The less powerful party, in accepting the more powerful one's protection, is obliged to meet the conditions laid down. We find such promises and obligations in the Book of Exodus: God promises protection and the Promised Land (23:20); God promises personal relationship with the people of Israel (19:5—6), and the people promise to show their faithfulness to the agreement by obeying God's laws (24:7).

This solemn agreement between God and the people together with the experience of deliverance comprise the foundational religious experience of Moses and of the Hebrew people: Moses, a sensitive and faithful person, recognizes and accepts a call from God. Through his leadership, all the people encounter God in the midst of their experiences as refugees. God frees them from oppression, leads them to safety and promises to continue to relate to them in a special way. A solemn agreement recognizes this relationship.

This is an experience of God active in history, freeing and choosing a people. Social and political experiences become religious events, a time of revelation. Gradually the experience would be told and retold in symbolic stories and expressed in rituals. Much later all this would be written down. Still later, deliverance and covenant would provide the formative religious tradition for Jesus.

Pause and reflect on your own experience. How well can you identify with Moses' experience of God?

The Experience of Jesus

As we did with Moses and the Jewish people, so now we ask about Jesus' experience of something more: "Jesus of Nazareth, what happened in your life? What was your experience of God?"

Almost all our knowledge of Jesus comes from the community that was founded on him. Thus, we can discover Jesus' experience only by listening to what the Christian community said about him in the Scriptures. And the Scriptures, of course, are accounts of faith. The New

Testament, like the Old Testament, has a purpose: to tell us of God's action in the world, not to give an exact historical or scientific account of events. In telling the story of Jesus, the Christian community included its faith perspective in the very details of the story, just as Exodus has Moses give details about menus and celebrations.

A few dates will be helpful in interpreting the stories about Jesus. The four Gospels were not written down until long after Jesus' death (about 30 A.D.). After his death and resurrection, those who had come to believe in him began telling their story to others. (The next chapter will trace the development of the early Christian community in greater detail.) These stories recalled teachings and events in Jesus' life. Some of these accounts may have been written; others were handed on orally. The first Gospel we have today (Mark) was not written until some 40 years after Jesus' death—that is, about 70 A.D.. In the next 10 to 20 years, the Gospels of Matthew and Luke were written. Both are based on Mark's Gospel together with other sources. John's Gospel wasn't written in its present form until the end of the first century. The oldest New Testament writings are Paul's letters, composed in the 50's and 60's A.D..

As we turn to the Gospels to reflect on Jesus' life, then, we must deal with various layers of Christian experience and composition. The top layer is the Gospels, which are edited, rewritten and theologically interpreted accounts about Jesus. The middle layer is an oral and written tradition made up of stories and anecdotes remembered by a particular community and handed on in a creative tradition shaped by community concerns. Finally, at the bottom is the material out of which a profile of the historical Jesus can be constructed.

One more caution: Many of us already hold firm convictions about the life of Jesus. We may need to work at hearing what is being said here. Certain presuppositions and conclusions may be different!

One of these convictions is a central element of the Christian faith: the belief that Jesus was both divine and human. This conviction is clearly expressed in the New Testament. We must remember, of course, that the Gospels were written from a post-resurrection perspective. The new insight and understanding which result from the resurrection experience color the way the stories are told—particularly since their very purpose is expressing faith! Thus the divinity of Jesus is affirmed throughout the Gospels, even to his preexistence as the Word (see John 1:1-18).

For those of us who come almost 2,000 years later, faith in Jesus' divinity is taken for granted. Indeed, many of us may find it easier to believe that Jesus was God than to accept that he was truly a man.

But in our attempt to appreciate Jesus' experience of revelation, we must try to get behind these faith statements to the experiences themselves. We want to know what happened to Jesus and what led his disciples to claim that he was God in the first place.

Our own experience of Jesus is just about the opposite from the disciples' experience of him. The disciples first encountered a human being, Jesus of Nazareth. Only gradually—indeed, not until after the resurrection—would they recognize and proclaim his divinity. To appreciate fully Jesus' and the disciples' experiences, we must try to follow that same path.

Of course we are dealing here with mystery, a human being who is also divine. While we cannot really explain what it means to be divine, we do know what it means to be human. So we can start at this point in our pondering of Jesus' life. Jesus was human. He had to face the same basic realities of life that we do: love and friendship, discouragement and loss, ignorance and pain, joy and trust. Jesus had to eat and drink; he had to learn and figure out how he was to live his life.

Yes, this implies that Jesus did not know the future. To be truly human, Jesus had to search for meaning as we all do. The Christian faith proclaims that Jesus was indeed truly and fully human (in every way except sin). Therefore, whatever we know of our human condition we can safely attribute to Jesus.

How, then, does Jesus' divinity fit in? Perhaps by not interfering with his being fully human. For any interference—such as divine foreknowledge explicitly operative in Jesus' human consciousness—would rob Jesus of his humanity. He would not then truly be like one of us. True, the Scriptures seem to tell the story otherwise and emphasize the divinity; that is why it is so important to remember *when* they were written (after the resurrection) and *why* (to proclaim Jesus as Lord and Savior).

Another dimension of Jesus' life was his experience of religion. Moses' story and the story of the people of Israel was Jesus' story. As he grew, Jesus listened to and prayed with the Hebrew Scriptures. He pondered the lives of Abraham and Moses, of Jeremiah and Isaiah. Their God was Jesus' God—a God who continued to be active in the people's life, freeing and choosing and calling them back to the covenant. This Jewish context, then, nurtured Jesus' knowledge of and relationship with God.

We can also gain insight into Jesus' experience of God by looking at Jesus' activities and teachings as described in the Gospels. Of course the four Gospels present four very different portraits of Jesus. Because of the limits of space and time, we will concentrate on just one: Luke's Gospel. In attempting to answer our question, "Jesus, what was your experience of God?" we will pay special attention to Jesus' experience of *Abba* (a word which implies an intimate, loving relationship) and to Jesus' understanding of the Reign of God.

'Abba'

Scholars have helped us to appreciate the significance of Jesus' use of *Abba* as his term for addressing God. Jesus chose a word which small children used to address their fathers. *Abba* is best translated "Daddy"; it conveys a sense of childlike simplicity and familiarity. "Father," as we say in the Lord's Prayer, is actually too formal a translation.

It would have been unusual for an adult Jew of Jesus' time to address God in this affectionate way. That the Christian community continued to use this word in telling its story about Jesus is a good indication, scholars tell us, that this was actually the way Jesus addressed God.

Abba is important for our consideration of Jesus' experience because it points to a very intimate, loving relationship between God and Jesus. How did it develop? We have no way of answering in detail, but we can assume that this bond developed gradually as Jesus lived life, read the Hebrew Scriptures, asked himself about his own response to God, listened to John the Baptist, and began his own prophetic ministry, taking time to be alone and to pray. The God of Abraham, Isaac, Jacob, Moses, Isaiah, Jeremiah was Abba to Jesus.

We catch another glimpse into Jesus' experience of God in the parables. One of the most helpful is Luke 15:11-32—often called the Parable of the Prodigal Son. This parable about the possibility of reconciliation is better described, however, as the Parable of the Forgiving Father. The details are familiar: The younger son demands his inheritance, leaves home, spends all the money and finally returns to his father's house, asking to be treated as a servant. Notice the actions of the father: he allows his son freedom even to waste the inheritance; he watches for his return; he forgives the son without any bitterness, throwing a party to celebrate; he goes out to console the angry older brother. In this parable Jesus is telling us a lot about his own experience of God. Abba is a loving, forgiving, gentle parent. Jesus evidently feels very close to this personal God, a God who reaches out to all, both those who wander away and those who stay at home.

If we look closely at the events and teachings of Jesus' life, we see that Jesus focused his energies neither on himself nor on the Church. Jesus' whole life was directed to Abba—and to the Reign of God.

The Reign of God

The Reign of God is a central image in the Gospels. Simply put, the Reign means that God's power is at work in a particular situation. God's saving presence is found there. The Reign (also called Kingdom or Sovereignty) does not imply a particular place or time; the Reign is present whenever and wherever God's loving presence is manifested. Therefore the Reign may exist in individual persons, in institutions and in the whole world. The miracles of Jesus are symbols of God's Reign breaking into our world, of healing and salvation overcoming brokenness and sin.

Jesus used parables to speak about the Reign of God. Although he thus risked being misunderstood, Jesus allowed his listeners to make the connection between what he was talking about and what they were already expecting. He usually upset many of their preconceived notions of God's righteousness and power. Yet he took a chance that his words would touch the people in their depths and that they would act upon this discovery. He did so because he believed that the Reign of God, so evident in his own experience, could—and would—be recognized by others.

At times Jesus began his parables with the statement, "The Reign of God is like...." At other times, this statement is only implied. In Luke 8:4-15, for instance, Jesus simply begins, "A farmer went out to sow some seed," and goes on to describe the different types of ground on which the seed fell. Part of *our* need in hearing this parable is to recognize that Jesus is describing very poor farming techniques. His hearers at the time, of course, knew that; they also knew that even the best techniques of the day produced about sevenfold. But in the parable the rich soil produces a hundredfold. Jesus is telling his listeners how surprising God's Reign is, how overflowing in goodness—not sevenfold but a hundredfold!

A similar parable can also be misunderstood because we do not know specifics from Jesus' day. In Luke 13:20-21, Jesus describes a woman mixing yeast into three measures of flour. Most of us miss the heart of Jesus' teaching because we do not know that three "measures" of flour is enough for 50 pounds of bread! Some years ago in an *I Love Lucy* episode, Lucy was baking bread and this huge loaf just kept rising and coming out of the oven, finally pinning her against the kitchen wall. Most of us would never think of Jesus as the original scriptwriter for Lucille Ball, but that exaggeration is the heart of the parable. The Reign of God is full of joy and surprise and goodness.

Because of Jesus' intimate relationship with God as Abba, Jesus experienced the presence of the Reign in and through his own life. And what he tried to tell others in his parables is that they could experience this Reign too!

Another section of Luke which provides rich insight into Jesus' experience of God's loving and saving presence is what we commonly know as the Sermon on the Mount (although the location in Luke's Gospel is level ground—see Luke 6:17-49; cf. Matthew 5:1—7:29). In this collection of Jesus' teachings we discover some of the surprise and goodness of the Reign: The hungry will be satisifed; those who weep now will laugh; those who are poor will be part of the Reign. The Sermon also gives other characteristics of life in the Reign: love of enemies, generosity, compassion, forgiveness, humility and authentic action. And, as is typical of Luke's Gospel, we also hear about the dangers of wealth and complacency.

Jesus' Life

We can also deepen our appreciation of Jesus' religious experience—his experience of something more—by looking at events of his life such as his baptism (Luke 3:1-22). The conclusion of the baptism story states, "When all the people were baptized, and Jesus was at prayer after likewise being baptized, the skies opened and the Holy Spirit descended on him in visible form like a dove. A voice from heaven was heard to say: 'You are my beloved Son. On you my favor rests'" (3:21-22).

Did the sky really part and did a voice boom from heaven? That is the same kind of wrong question as "Was the bush really burning?" And the answer is also the same: The Scriptures were not written to give this kind of information. Although we cannot say that it definitely never happened, our experience indicates that the sky does not open, the Holy Spirit is not a bird, and voices do not suddenly speak from the heavens.

We can and do, however, experience an awareness of our mission in life—our vocation. So it is likely that Luke is trying to describe with symbols Jesus' early sense of his own mission and of his special relationship with *Abba*. Such an understanding clearly fits with what we have been discussing in this chapter: the true humanity of Jesus and his intimate relationship with God.

Other Gospel events can be understood in a similar way. Only two sources in the New Testament describe the birth of Jesus: Luke is one (1:1—2:52); Matthew is the other (1:1—2:23).

But the two stories are very, very different in their details. Because most of us have combined the two stories in our hearts and minds, we realize these differences only by looking carefully at the two accounts. Matthew focuses on Joseph, has Mary and Joseph living in Bethlehem, and includes the magi and the flight into Egypt. Luke focuses on Mary, has Mary and Joseph living in Nazareth (going to Bethlehem only for the Roman census), and includes the shepherds and a peaceful visit to Jerusalem. Once again, we must avoid asking the wrong question: Which way did it happen?

In his extensive study of the infancy narratives, *The Birth of the Messiah*, Raymond Brown emphasizes that what is important is the religious message of the stories. What is this message? Brown claims it is twofold: to proclaim the identity of Jesus as truly God and truly human and to show how Jesus is linked to and fulfills the Hebrew Scriptures. Brown states that each infancy narrative is in fact, the whole gospel in miniature: The full identity of Jesus (divine and human) is revealed; this good news is shared with others and accepted by some (shepherds, magi, Simeon, Anna) but rejected by others (Herod the king, the chief priests and scribes). Understood in this way, the story of Jesus' birth affirms this chapter's insights into the experience of Jesus and in no way contradicts them.

Jesus' Passion, Death and Resurrection

Let's now look at the central event of Jesus' life: his passion, death and resurrection (Luke 22:1—24:53). The longest single section of any Gospel is the story of Jesus' passion and death. Scholars point out that this part of the Gospel was the first to take shape within the early Christian community. As with the infancy accounts, we tend to combine the different passion narratives in our hearts and minds. Still, there are significant differences in the four portraits. For example, Mark describes Jesus as abandoned by his disciples, rejected by the crowd and seemingly forsaken by his God. But John describes Jesus as being in control, freely laying down his life and dying in a sovereign and life-giving manner. (See Raymond Brown's *A Crucified Christ in Holy Week* for a detailed comparison.) Thus even the passion accounts, while rooted in a historical fact (the crucifixion), are stories of faith in which theology, not biography, determines which events are narrated.

What, then, are some of the specific brush strokes in Luke's portrait of the passion? Luke invites his hearer not so much to adore Jesus as Son of God (John's portrait) nor to learn about him (Matthew's) nor to look on the scene in overwhelming sorrow (Mark's), but simply to be with Jesus. Luke invites the hearer to become another Simon of Cyrene helping Jesus carry his cross, another Peter recognizing weakness, another good thief expressing hope.

Luke's passion story continues to emphasize the same characteristics and experiences of Jesus found throughout the Gospel. Jesus is not overwhelmed with fear and agony but prays in the garden and calmly faces death, just as he steadfastly journeyed toward Jerusalem in the prior narrative. Jesus heals the high priest's slave as he healed so many during his ministry. Jesus consoles the "daughters of Jerusalem" and forgives those who crucified him, in the same way he described mercy and tenderness in his parables and expressed them in his actions. Finally, as he dies, Jesus continues to express his profound trust in Abba; his last words are, "Father, into your hands, I commend my spirit" (Luke 23:46b).

This trust is in striking contrast to the abandonment expressed in Mark 15:34 and Matthew 27:47: "My God, my God, why have you forsaken me?" It is different from the sovereign control and triumph expressed in John: "Jesus, realizing that everything was now finished, said to fulfill the Scripture..." (19:28) and "Now it is finished." (19:30). Jesus' intimate, loving relationship with Abba sustains him even in death.

But the passion and death are only the beginning of Jesus' glorification. The resurrection completes this central event. In the descriptions of the resurrection we find much symbolic language: dazzling lights, appearances sudden as a flash, a mysterious inability to recognize Jesus but then ecstatic joy with the recognition, a sudden fading away. All this reminds us that the resurrection is a different kind of reality, not the same kind of historical event as the crucifixion.

The resurrection is an experience in faith, known and

proclaimed by the disciples but denied by unbelievers. The disciples experienced Jesus as alive in a new way. (We will talk more about this in the next chapter.) His presence transformed them and their world. How else can one describe such an experience except with symbolic language?

The resurrection can be understood as God's affirmation of Jesus' faithfulness. His intimate, loving relationship is now confirmed by *Abba*'s power which raises Jesus to new life. The definitive triumph of life over death takes place in Jesus' resurrection.

Pause and reflect on your own experience. What convictions about Jesus do you hold? How has your concept of him changed over the years?

Summing Up

In Jesus' experience of Abba, in his parables and in the events of his life, we see a profound example of the experience of revelation. And yet Jesus' life is not altogether different from our own. In fact, if we accept his humanity, we can see the continuity between his life and ours. Although his life would become a source of revelation for many, Jesus himself had to experience life and God in ways just like us.

Jesus was, therefore, part of the Jewish banyan tree, nourished by the Hebrew Scriptures and rituals, believing in one God who was active in history, choosing and freeing the people of Israel. But as a source of new revelation, Jesus himself become a new banyan tree. His life, death and resurrection provide a source of new life for others.

We who are Christians are all part of this tree. In the earlier chapters of this book, we have seen that we are new roots, emerging from the branches and perhaps still dangling or perhaps beginning to root. The branches of symbols and stories are essential for nourishing us, for keeping us connected to the main trunk, Jesus. In the next chapter we will consider more branches—some of the oldest, in fact—which sprouted from the trunk, Jesus. These are the branches not only of Scripture but also of ritual and community.

For discussion and reflection:

1) Compare Moses' call to the call of some modern religious leader. What similarities can you find? Can you trace the same threads through the story of Jesus' baptism? In your own call?

2) How does Judaism communicate the experience of the exodus to new generations? How does the Hebrew experience of covenant relate to the Christian experience of the New Covenant?

3) Does the "post-resurrection perspective" of the Gospels help or hinder your understanding of Jesus?

4) Recall your favorite parables, your favorite scene in Jesus' life. What do they tell you about Jesus' experience of God, about the Reign of God? Relate them to the Sermon on the Mount.

CHAPTER FIVE

More Branches:
Understanding Organized Religion

Based on the foundational experiences of Moses and the Hebrews and of Jesus and his disciples, Judaism and Christianity grew and developed. In this chapter we will look at the process which begins with the experience of revelation—the encounter with God and the resulting insight into the meaning of life—and moves to the formation of an institution which remembers and hands on that experience.

Let's begin by reflecting on some basic stages in the movement from personal religious experience to institutionalized religion. Then we will be able to see with greater clarity the details of the development of Judaism and Christianity.

Institutionalizing Revelation

In *Principles of Christian Theology* the contemporary Anglican theologian John Macquarrie offers a helpful analysis of the steps leading to organized religion: God's initiative; human response; expressing the revelation in words; expressing the revelation in actions; a communal dimension.

God's Initiative: Revelation

First of all, the beginning of religion belongs to God and God's initiative in the world. Our first consideration of experiencing "something more" in nature or love or tragedy emphasized God's involvement in the experience, even though God's activity is from within and therefore not always easy to discern. Indeed, perhaps many of us still feel that it would be easier to identify God if burning bushes did speak and voices did boom from heaven, but our study so far has shown that God need not act this way in order to be truly present. God's initiative is primary—whether in the life of Moses or of Jesus or in our own lives. Organized religion, then, is rooted in the experience of revelation—which is always experienced as "gift."

Human Response: Faith

God takes the initiative, but then some kind of response is called for. We saw in Chapter 2 that humans can choose either to be open to something more or to cut themselves off from the divine. This openness, this acceptance of God's invitation, we call *faith*. A positive response continues the dialogue begun by God—indeed, allows the communication to *be* a dialogue. Faith is the whole person accepting God's presence and saying yes to God's activity in the world.

The process of God's initiative and human response is exactly what we have been reflecting upon throughout this book. It is the experience of something more; it is the experience of revelation. Thus the Hebrews found God in their refugee experience, the one God who was freeing and saving them. They said yes to this God in their acceptance of the covenant. Jesus experienced Abba as intimately close and loving. He responded by being faithful to his call, even to accepting death on a cross.

Usually such an experience of God will simply lead the individual either to join a particular religion or to deepen an already existing commitment. Only rarely does it lead to the formation of a new religion, as happened for the Hebrews and for Jesus' disciples. But whether in an old or new religion, such an experience leads to outward expression in words, actions and social relationships. These outward expressions, essential for us as human beings, make up Macquarrie's final three phases of organized religion. Even though they may take place simultaneously, we will consider them separately.

Expression in Words: Symbol and Story

How natural it is for us to want to share good news with others, especially our friends but sometimes anyone nearby! So it is with the experience of revelation. As we saw in Chapter 3, symbolic stories have always been a favorite means for trying to communicate the depth of religious experience. Thus, myth emerges as the first stage of expressing the experience of revelation and faith in words. Recall, for example, how the Hebrews told their story of the encounter with God on Mount Sinai (Exodus 19:16-20).

As religion develops over time and within a particular culture, the expression of the experience in words also develops. Once myths take shape, people begin extracting from them central beliefs and doctrines. These may well be expressed in creeds or other short summaries of what the religion holds. The process of searching for a better understanding and articulation of the foundational experience continues with the development of theology. This discipline uses all forms of knowledge (philosophy, the human and natural sciences) in its attempt to clarify revelation and faith. This stage (as we saw in Chapter 3) does not replace the earlier stages of myth and creed, but supplements them.

In Christianity, for example, we see in the Scriptures the belief that Jesus is both divine and human. This faith is proclaimed in the Nicene Creed, and theologians continue even today trying to express this mystery. As is evident, then, the expression of the original experience in words is a complex process, but a process which is absolutely necessary for the remembering and handing on of this experience.

Expression in Actions: Ritual and Ethics

The experience of revelation and faith are expressed in two distinct forms of action: rituals and ethical living. At the same time a people speak their myths, they also use symbolic gestures to embody the experience. Ordinary events take on a deeper meaning; for example, special meals can become a sacred action. Various names are given these symbolic actions: *ritual, ceremony, liturgy.*

The experience of God is not limited just to certain

occasions, however. Its influence is felt and expressed in all areas of living. The experience of God changes the way people live their lives (we saw this in Maslow's description of peak experiences). When this influence is spelled out in detailed form, religion produces a series of laws or ethical systems.

The Communal Dimension: Structure and Authority

The experience of revelation is indeed a profoundly personal experience. Yet it presupposes and leads to community. Even the rare experiences of revelation which become the basis of new religions are grounded in some kind of communal tradition. Jesus and his first followers, for example, were rooted in their Jewish heritage. This heritage helped them to experience and express the breakthrough in their perception of religious meaning.

This type of religious experience also leads to the formation of a new community. Moses and Jesus were both able to express their experiences in ways which attracted other people and enabled them to enter into the experience. In this way, communities developed and became the privileged place for preserving the experience. In order to enter into the originating experience, new generations have to rely on these communities as they tell and retell their stories and act and reenact their sacred rituals. We see, then, that the community is valuable and necessary from the first experience of revelation.

For us Americans, this aspect of religion may be the most difficult to appreciate fully. We are very much a part of a culture which emphasizes the individual; therefore we find it difficult to accept the community as necessary and central.

Yet contemporary thought stresses this social dimension of our existence. To be human is to be in relationship with others. In *Building the Human*, Robert Johann dramatically makes this point by stating that no individual exists without an "other" who takes account of the person and for whom the individual's free response means something. Thus, religion must be social and interpersonal. Macquarrie highlights this insight by claiming that private faiths and religions are defective because they lack the communal dimension that is part of the very essence of being human.

The Risk of Corruption

Let's spend a little more time with these outward expressions of the experience of revelation. These expressions are actually the beginnings of organized religion. They are also absolutely necessary if the experience of God is to be shared with other human beings. Without external words and gestures, we would never have known of Moses and the Hebrews, of Jesus and the disciples. If the experience is never articulated for others to respond to, then no one else will ever know about it. The experience will die with the individual. Therefore, expressing the experience in words, in actions and in community is necessary and good.

It is also dangerous. Is *dangerous* too strong a word? Probably not. For history demonstrates again and again that in all religions the externals become absolutized. What starts out as a means (words and gestures to communicate the experience) becomes an end. The specific story or ritual or community structure becomes the one and only way of expressing the revelation and faith. As a result, something that was appropriate for a particular time and culture becomes frozen; people attempt to make this expression fit all times and cultures. There can be so much emphasis on one particular *expression* that the originating *experience* is neglected or even lost. This is a very great danger indeed.

We have already seen some of the problems associated with myths and their proper interpretation. (see pp. 50-51) The same is true for creeds, dogmas and theologies. Any of these verbal expressions is necessarily rooted in a certain time and culture and worldview which limit the statement's adaptability. Because the experience of revelation is always more than can be contained in words, one perspective will never be sufficient for all times and places.

For example, given the philosophy and especially the polemics of the Reformation, the term *transubstantiation* seems to have been an appropriate attempt to clarify the meaning of the Eucharist. Now, more than 400 years later, given different philosophies and insights, *transubstantiation* may no longer be the best explanation of the Eucharist. The reality is the same (the Eucharist), but our expressions can and often must change.

Vatican II said it this way: "The deposit of faith or revealed truths are one thing; the manner in which they are formulated without violence to their meaning and significance is another" (*Pastoral Constitution on the Church in the Modern World*, #62). The danger is that the "manner" will be canonized even at the risk of no longer handing on the faith. Blind assent to creed or dogma then replaces living faith.

The same problem faces expression in actions. What was once a fitting symbolic action may not make sense in different times and cultures. For most people the change from Latin Masses to English allowed for greater participation and understanding, and so led to better community worship. Symbolic gestures which may "work" for some of us in the United States may well need other forms to be effective among minority groups in the U.S., not to mention in Africa, for example. Again the danger is to hold on to any one form of expression, as if the deeper reality were tied to that expression ("God can only be worshiped in Latin").

It is important to note, however, that new does not necessarily mean better. Careful study is always a required part of change; otherwise the most important point, the authentic expression of revelation and faith, will once again be neglected. And when the experience of God is lost, then symbolic actions become mere magical gestures or empty ritual.

Corruptions resulting from religion's communal dimension are both varied and widespread. The existence of the community demands some structure. Yet power and authority are all too frequently abused. Individuals and institutions alike seek power for its own sake. Churches make questionable alliances with the politically powerful to gain wealth and success. Happiness and even lives are sacrificed to the structure. Large parts of the community are neglected or even oppressed. Just within the history of Christianity we find corrupt and authoritarian popes and bishops, colonialism and persecutions, clericalism and sexism. The list could go on and on.

This frank acknowledgement of the dangers of organized

religion in no way undermines its importance. It does recognize the ambiguity of religion and the need to acknowledge both together—religion's value and necessity and its tendency toward corruption.

In the rest of this chapter, we will focus on the goodness of institutionalization. Looking at the experiences of Moses and of Jesus as our case studies, we will see how religions grew naturally from the desire to share these experiences. We will see how the external expressions preserved the originating experience of God and allow us to enter that experience in our own day. In the next chapter, we will return to the other half of the ambiguity, the corrupting trends in religion, and consider the ongoing need for renewal and reform.

From Moses to Judaism

In the last chapter we attempted to get some sense of Moses' and the Hebrews' experience of God: As they fled Egypt, the Hebrews found that it was not by their own power or even by Moses' leadership that they were being saved. It was the one God, Yahweh, who freed them, leading them in the Exodus and choosing them to be God's very own.

After fleeing Egypt, the Hebrews wandered in the desert and eventually settled in the Promised Land, where their history was to be one of growth and then decline, exile and resettlement. Again and again they would drift away from the covenant, often getting involved in the worship of other gods. Again and again, they would be called back to faithfulness to the covenant. Through hundreds of years, deliverance-covenant provided the basis of their religion. The people of Israel told and retold their story of God's action, and they celebrated it in festivals. We see clearly Macquarrie's five stages of religion. God's initiative in deliverance and the people's positive response in covenant form the foundation of Judaism. This encounter with God is told in story form and eventually written down in the Scriptures; it is expressed in ritual and formed into laws; it creates and is remembered in community.

By looking at the community's stories, we can appreciate how liturgy and laws embodied the original experience of God and so allowed new generations to enter into this experience. Let's return to Exodus 12, where we find many details for the celebration of Passover: an unblemished one-year-old sheep or goat; roasted meat eaten with unleavened bread and bitter herbs; sandals and staff ready for the journey. These details, of course, represent the actual liturgical celebrations of later Israel, now read back into the Exodus event itself.

We have already seen how it was natural for the community to gather at its festivals to retell its most important story, and to express this story in rituals. Thus, the meal itself becomes a privileged way not only to recall a past event (the encounter with God in the exodus), but also to provide the context in which that encounter may be experienced once again. So the details of the meal have symbolic importance and allow later generations of Jews to enter into the Passover experience. In this way, the ritual actualizes (makes real and present) God's saving actions of deliverance and choice. Reread Exodus 12:24-27, which tells the Hebrew teenager why the ritual is so significant! The power of the ritual is rooted not in magic, but in the reality of symbol and in the faith of the community.

We have also seen that the Ten Commandments were given in the context of the covenant (Exodus 19—20). God promised to be their God, and the people promised to obey all of Yahweh's commands. The significance of this context for our understanding of law should not be missed. In its roots, the law is something very precious for Judaism. The law is intimately linked with the covenant; indeed, the law shows the people how to be faithful to God. Observance of the law is perfection. Therefore, the law expresses God's will for them and provides their true identity. Listen to Psalm 19:

The law of the LORD is perfect,
  refreshing the soul;
The decree of the LORD is trustworthy,
  giving wisdom to the simple.
The precepts of the LORD are right,

rejoicing the heart;
The command of the LORD is clear,
    enlightening the eye;
The fear of the LORD is pure,
    enduring forever;
The ordinances of the LORD are true,
    all of them just;
They are more precious than gold,
    than a heap of purest gold;
Sweeter also than syrup
    or honey from the comb. (Psalm 19:8-11)

Probably few of us would describe law with such praise. Yet if we can get some feel for the conviction expressed in Psalm 19, then we will be able to appreciate the great value and function of Torah (law) in the Jewish experience. Indeed, Torah implies the whole way of covenant existence in which God's will is found. (For another account of the giving of the law, see Deuteronomy 5:1—11:32.)

We can see, then, that both liturgy and law are central in forming Judaism as a religion and in preserving it. Liturgy and law remember God's saving actions and make the encounter with God present wherever and whenever the ritual is celebrated and the law lived. Because the people of Israel were always tempted to adopt the religious practices of foreign nations (and so worship other gods and break the covenant), many laws were formulated to protect the rituals and to describe authentic worship. Not surprisingly, much of the Pentateuch is devoted to this task. (For a few examples, see Exodus 20:22—23:19 and Exodus 34:1-35.)

Law and liturgy, story and community are absolutely necessary for Judaism. When we reflected upon the characteristics of organized religion earlier in this chapter, we also acknowledged that these outward expressions tend to become corrupted, so it has been in Judaism. A long list of reformers (from the prophets to the Pharisees to Reform Judaism) have attempted to find more appropriate and timely means to express deliverance and covenant. But this need for reform in no way undermines the necessity and value of the

91

institution—of the expression of the experience in words, in actions and in community.

Pause and reflect on your own experience. What role do law, liturgy, story and community play in your experience of religion?

From Jesus to Christianity

Let's turn now to our other case study, Jesus. His life, death and resurrection were a source of revelation for his disciples and became the foundation of a new religion, Christianity. As we saw in Chapter 4, Jesus' public life centered neither on himself nor on the Church but on Abba and Abba's Reign. Rooted in this intimate, loving relationship, Jesus wanted to help others recognize God's saving presence. But his life and preaching inevitably led to conflict (as had been the case for so many of the prophets before him) and finally to execution. During his life, Jesus must have considered this possibility. He knew the destiny of previous prophets and, in his own time, that of John the Baptist. He had to be aware of the growing tension between his mission and the political-religious leaders. Yet, because of his trust in Abba, Jesus remained faithful to that mission. Thus we can see that his death cannot be separated from the events of his public ministry, but resulted from those acts. Jesus' death was not something he went out of his way to choose in some inhuman manner.

But the crucifixion was not the end of the story. Jesus was raised on the third day; his trust in Abba was confirmed. The resurrection surely was the pivotal experience in the life of the disciples.

They had become powerfully attracted to this Jesus of Nazareth. They had witnessed his deeds and listened to his teachings. More and more they felt that their hopes for a political messiah, rooted in their Jewish heritage, would be fulfilled in Jesus. How crushing, then, the crucifixion must have been. All their hopes and expectations were shattered. Their leader was executed as a common criminal.

But the resurrection transformed everything. Jesus was alive in a new way. Gradually the disciples came to see more clearly; they reflected on their experiences of Jesus in light of their Scriptures—the Hebrew Scriptures. Inspired by the Spirit, they began to tell their story. Surely the resurrection was not an event they could prove. Yet it had transformed them and the world. And so the only evidence they could present for the truth of their story was their own lives, the hope and love, trust and joy that they experienced and shared.

Much is contained in this brief description of Jesus' death and resurrection. First it recalls Jesus' own experience of revelation, his special relationship with Abba. But we are also looking at the *disciples'* experience of revelation. They encountered Jesus of Nazareth as a very special person. But it was not until after the resurrection that they could begin to put the pieces together. Only then were they able to recognize that they had met God in Jesus.

What does this dramatic claim mean? We know that we cannot meet God as God, for God is always transcendent—that is, something more, beyond human encounters. What the disciples proclaimed was that to meet Jesus was to experience a personal encounter with the transcendent God—because of who Jesus was. In Jesus, in a unique way, people were brought into contact with God in a way that transformed their lives. In Jesus, people met God; indeed, they said, Jesus *is* divine.

Still more is contained in our few paragraphs! They describe not only the experiences of Jesus and of the disciples but also the beginnings of a new religion. As a result of their experience, the disciples (that is, all those who experienced the risen Jesus) began to tell their story. The Acts of the Apostles describes these beginnings, again with the use of symbolic stories. First, Acts describes the process of replacing Judas and the criteria to be used in the selection. "It is entirely fitting therefore, that one of those who was of our company while the Lord Jesus moved among us, from the baptism of John until the day he was taken up from us, should be named as witness with us to his resurrection" (1:21-22). Hear the emphasis on the historical experience (having been with Jesus), on the central importance of the resurrection and on the role of the disciples as witness.

Acts goes on to describe this witness by giving an example of Peter's preaching (2:14-36). Peter situates his proclamation in the Jewish context by recalling various passages from the Hebrew Scriptures; then he summarizes the story of Jesus, focusing on his death and resurrection. Peter concludes with this statement: "Therefore let the whole house of Israel know beyond any doubt that God has made both Lord and Messiah this Jesus whom you crucified" (2:36). The resurrection faith is boldly proclaimed; Jesus is truly human and truly divine.

Before continuing our investigation into these beginnings of organized Christianity, let's pull together a few key points. Jesus' life, death and resurrection are clearly the starting point of everything. Jesus is best understood as the foundation of Christianity. Jesus preached about *Abba*; only after the resurrection did Jesus himself become the center of the disciples' preaching (as in Peter's proclamation in Acts 2). Thus, the preacher became the one preached about.

It was the disciples who actually built on this foundation: They did the preaching; they did the traveling; they began the process of institutionalization. Paul expresses this insight well:

> After all, who is Apollos? And who is Paul? Simply ministers through whom you became believers, each of them doing only what the Lord assigned him. I planted the seed and Apollos watered it, but God made it grow…. Thanks to the favor God showed me I laid a foundation as a wise master-builder might do, and now someone else is building upon it. Everyone, however, must be careful how he builds. No one can lay a foundation other than the one that has been laid, namely Jesus Christ….Are you not aware that you are the temple of God, and that the Spirit of God dwells in you? If anyone destroys God's temple, God will destroy him. For the temple of God is holy, and you are that temple.
>
> (1 Corinthians 3:5-6, 10-12, 16-17)

Here, then, we see examples of Macquarrie's basic characteristics of institutionalization at work. Jesus encountered God as *Abba* and responded faithfully throughout his ministry, even to death. Jesus, of course, used words and actions to communicate his experience of God, and a community of disciples developed—all within the context of Judaism. But these disciples, in turn, experienced God in and through Jesus. There was new revelation and new faith as the disciples came to recognize and accept Jesus as Lord. And there were new expressions, too, as the disciples turned first to other Jews and then to Gentiles to proclaim and celebrate the Good News.

Before we look more carefully at those new expressions in word, in ritual and in community, however, one more comment about the disciples must be made. Those women and men who experienced the risen Jesus were limited in number. Exactly what their experience of the risen Jesus was we cannot say (the Scriptures use very symbolic language to describe the situations), but scholars do point out that these experiences stopped. Jesus is described as ascending into heaven, and Pentecost symbolizes the experience of God's presence in a new way. It should be remembered that Paul claims to be an apostle, that is, one who encountered the risen Lord. Thus, while the experiences of the risen Jesus probably happened over a longer period of time than 40 days (because biblical scholars can date Paul's conversion), still the number of eyewitnesses was limited. Keeping this significant factor in mind, so let us now trace the development of the early Christian community in more detail.

The Development of the Christian Community

The Acts of the Apostles is the second volume of Luke's two-volume work (the first is Luke's Gospel). Therefore, to read either the Gospel or Acts is to read only half a book; to appreciate the whole story we must read both. In his second volume, Luke continues the major theme of his Gospel: that the Good News of Jesus is intended for all peoples, Jews and Gentiles. The spread of this Good News is the work of the Spirit within and through the community. Luke presents an idyllic view, again giving us a religious message not an exact historical account. Still, a careful reading of Acts and of Paul's letters offers insight into the growth of the community and into the expression of revelation and faith in words and actions.

Luke develops his story in Acts around a geographical model. First he follows Peter in Jerusalem, his acts and his preaching. Later he switches focus to Paul as he travels to Asia Minor, to Greece and finally to Rome. As center of the empire, Rome symbolizes the whole known world. When the Good News reaches Rome, it reaches all the world.

In these preachings and travels, we find the beginnings of an organized religion. Those who experienced the risen Jesus begin to tell their story, first in Jerusalem and then in other cities (recall Acts 2:14-36; this type of scene is repeated again and again). As these disciples proclaimed the Word, other people came to believe in Jesus. Certainly not all the preaching was successful (see Acts 17:22-34), but the community of believers did grow. These new members had not witnessed Jesus as risen, but did experience the truth of the disciples' preaching. The community in Jerusalem stands as a symbol of these early Christian communities and is described in Acts in terms which are clearly idealized:

> The community of believers were of one heart and one mind. None of them ever claimed anything as his own; rather, everything was held in common. With power the apostles bore witness to the resurrection of the Lord Jesus, and great respect was paid to them all; nor was there anyone needy among them, for all who owned property or houses sold them and donated the proceeds. They used to lay them at the feet of the apostles to be distributed to everyone according to his need. (Acts 4:32-35)

In fact, all were not united, as we will discover below when we look at the debate about admitting Gentiles into the community (also see Acts 6:1-7).

Naturally the disciples had to spend some time in each particular city, gradually building up the community. The disciples moved on to another place only after a local leader had been determined for the new community. Two basic models were used in this selection: (1) simple appointment to the office ("In each church they installed presbyters and, with prayer and fasting, commended them to the Lord in whom they had put their faith," Acts 14:23); (2) acknowledgment of a special gift of the Spirit ("We have gifts that differ according to the favor bestowed on each of us. One's gift may be prophecy; its use should be in proportion to his faith. It may be the gift of ministry; it should be used for service. One who is a teacher should use his gift for teaching..."; see Romans 12:6, 7; also see 1 Corinthians 12:1-31). However chosen, the local leader was recognized as being subordinate to the disciple, yet having a vital role to play in the growth of the community. For the leader was the symbol of unity who presided at the liturgy and who was the primary teacher.

It is very important to notice here how the early Christian community developed and grew: by preaching. The disciples told others of their experience of the life, death and resurrection of Jesus. These other people accepted this word and experienced God's presence in a new way in this Christian message. Since everything depends on the preaching, we see the absolute necessity of authentic witnesses and the danger of false stories.

To be a Christian, then, is to accept the word of the first disciples. This word became the basic norm, and the local leader was responsible for preserving this word faithfully. This, of course, does not mean mere memorization, for we have already seen how the Gospels present different portraits of Jesus because of the influence and needs of the local community. Thus, creativity and faithfulness can be held together, and this task is one of the primary responsibilities of the local leaders (although the Spirit's presence in the whole community must also be emphasized—see 1 Corinthians 12).

In the beginning, when there were disputes, the community (local leader) could contact the disciple for help in resolving the disagreement. But as those who experienced the risen Lord died (remember, they were a limited number of people), some of the communities wrote down the disciple's testimony—as handed on and adapted to that community. In this way the authentic preaching of the disciples was recorded and became our Gospels.

As the recorded witness of the earliest disciples, some of these written accounts became the ultimate norm, the privileged story of Jesus. (A curious dynamic is found here: The local community is first formed through the disciples' preaching; this community remembers and hands on this story; but when the disciples' testimony is written down, it replaces the disciples as norm and so the local communities are subordinate to it!) Throughout this process, it was the conviction and experience of the early Christian community that this development was happening under the guidance of the Spirit (see, for example, Acts 1:1; 2:21; 10:19, 20, 44-48; 13:1-12; 15:28-29).

As the story of Jesus was being told and then written, and as communities were formed and developed basic structures, at the same time ritual was also developing. That is, the story was told not only in words but also in symbolic gestures (what we now call sacraments). The most important of these symbolic actions was the celebration of the Eucharist. Once again, a meal became a sacred meal. The people gathered to tell the story of Jesus and to break bread together. Acts presents this picture very simply: "They devoted themselves to the apostles' instruction and the communal life, to the breaking of bread and the prayers" (2:42).

Paul recalls Jesus' own life as the basis for the Eucharist and deals with problems that already appeared in the community's celebration: "Every time, then, you eat this bread and drink this cup, you proclaim the death of the Lord until he comes! This means that whoever eats the bread or drinks the cup of the Lord unworthily sins against the body and blood of the Lord" (1 Corinthians 11:26-27; see the entire passage, 11:17-34). The Gospels, of course, in various passages and especially in the Last Supper scenes, also present a Eucharisic theology.

The best description of the developing significance of the Eucharist, however, may well be in Luke 24:13-35, the story of the two disciples on the road to Emmaus. All we have to do is substitute the early Christian community for the two disciples and we find a wonderful description of this development.

The first stage is a retelling of the life, death and resurrection of Jesus. The second is the use of the Hebrew Scriptures. The first Christians were Jews, of course, so they turned to their Scriptures to shed light. The early community had to reread these Scriptures in light of their experience of Jesus, and they came to new insight into both their experience and the meaning of the Scriptures. For example, passages in Isaiah which described a suffering servant were seen in a new light and linked with Jesus' passion and death (see the "songs of the suffering servant," Isaiah 42:1-4; 49:1-7; 50:4-11; 52:13—53:12).

The third stage is the recognition of Jesus' presence in the breaking of the bread. The response is one of great joy ("Were not our hearts burning inside us..."; Luke 24:32) and of deep desire to share the Good News ("Then they recounted what had happened..."; Luke 24:35). Thus, in telling the story of Jesus, in reading Scripture and in breaking the bread, the early communities experienced Jesus' saving presence.

The other central symbolic gesture was Baptism. The early Christian community borrowed this ritual to express entrance into the community. This ritual of immersion symbolizes dying to the old life of sin and rising to a new life in Christ. In Acts almost every person or group who accepts the story of Jesus is baptized. For example, after hearing Peter's address on Pentecost the people ask: "'What are we to do, brothers?' Peter answered: 'You must reform and be baptized, each one of you, in the name of Jesus Christ, that your sins may be forgiven; then you will receive the gift of the Holy Spirit'" (Acts 2:37b-38). This pattern of repentance and belief and acceptance is repeated throughout Acts.

One issue in the development of the early community caused major turmoil: the admission of Gentiles into the community and whether they had to follow the Jewish law. This development is presented in Acts 10:1—15:35.

The section begins with the story of Peter and Cornelius, a Roman centurion. With wonderful symbols (angels, visions of food from heaven, voices) the story tells how the two men met and how Peter preached to Cornelius and his family. Peter proclaims to them, "You must know that it is not proper for a

Jew to associate with a Gentile or to have dealings with him. But God has made it clear to me that no one should call any man unclean and impure" (Acts 10:28). And, Peter adds, "I begin to see how true it is that God shows no partiality. Rather, the man of any nation who fears God and acts uprightly is acceptable to him" (Acts 10:34-35). Indeed, even as Peter told the story of Jesus, the Holy Spirit was poured out upon all who were listening. Acts goes on to describe some of Paul's works among the Gentiles. These accounts set the stage for the major confrontation which takes place in Jerusalem.

Some people demanded that Gentile Christians must be circumcised and follow the law of Moses. In Acts 15, the apostles and other leaders of the community meet to discuss the matter. Peter recalls his experience and states the resulting conviction that all peoples could believe in Jesus and that not all the details of the old law were necessary. Barnabas and Paul likewise describe their experiences. Finally, James decides in favor of admitting the Gentiles without forcing the Jewish law upon them (see Acts 15:19-21). The event represents a very significant transition: From this point on the Christian community becomes more and more distinct from its Jewish roots and moves from its Palestinian origins to openness to all peoples. (For another perspective on the whole debate, see Galatians 2:1-14.)

In these New Testament writings, we see the development of Christianity. We find all the basic characteristics of an organized religion: revelation and faith, expression in words, actions and community. Two points should be noted:

First, the development of organized Christianity was not according to some giant blueprint, not even according to some plan of Jesus. As we have clearly seen, Jesus centered his life around Abba and Abba's Reign. Christianity grew spontaneously out of Jesus' experience and the disciples' experience of the risen Jesus. They had good news which they wanted to share. So they did very human things: They tried to express their experience in stories and in rituals. They were convinced that all this was done under the direction of the Spirit. They evidently spoke with authority and expressed their experience well, for others listened and believed and experienced. And all this, often enough, was done under the threat of persecution and death (see Luke 21:5-38).

The second point is related to the first. The purpose of all the externals is to remember and to hand on the basic experience of revelation. Thus all the Scriptures and creeds and doctrines are important only insofar as they preserve and help us understand the life, death and resurrection of Jesus. All the rituals and moral codes are important only insofar as they help us to keep in touch with the revelation, to experience it anew in our own time and to embody it in our day-to-day lives. So too for the community: All its structure and authority are in service of the giving and receiving of revelation.

Pause and reflect on your own experience. How well have the externals of Christianity put you in touch with the experience of Jesus and the disciples?

Summing Up

As Macquarrie pointed out in the beginning of this chapter, the externals of religion are necessary if later generations are to enter into the original experience of revelation. Yet, as we will study in greater detail in the next chapter, all too often the externals become more important than the foundational experience. Even as the early Christian community had to struggle with change and reform, so too must the Church today be open to renewal in order faithfully to introduce new generations into the life, death and resurrection of Jesus.

In the last chapter, we saw that Jesus is the trunk of the Christian banyan tree. In this chapter we have investigated some of the major branches. We have looked carefully at the stories, rituals and community which are dependent on Jesus and which link new generations to him. The Christian tradition thus forms the major branches of the banyan tree which nourish us and connect us to our trunk.

For discussion and reflection:

1) Trace Macquarrie's five characteristics of religion through the religious tradition you know best. How necessary do the outward expressions (words, actions, community) seem?

2) Trace the corruption of Macquarrie's characteristics of religion through the tradition you know best. Is there still value in the tradition, or should the baby be thrown out with the bath water?

3) What does it mean to say that the power of ritual is rooted not in magic, but in the reality of symbol and the faith of the community? Relate this to your own experience of liturgy.

4) Discuss the importance of law in Judaism. Does law have a significant role in your religious tradition? In your personal life?

5) What does it mean to say that Jesus is the foundation of Christianity? How do you experience his life, death and resurrection in the Christian religious tradition? How do the problems of early Christianity shed some light on contemporary problems (e.g., ministry, authority)?

CHAPTER SIX

Pruning:
Choosing Renewal and Growth

Religion is ambiguous. As we have already seen, the outward expression of the experience of revelation and faith in words, action and community is both absolutely necessary and fraught with danger. Religion is necessary to preserve the experience for future generations, but it may also get separated from that experience and become corrupted. In the last chapter we focused on the value of religion in remembering and handing on the foundational revelation, especially the experiences of Moses and the Hebrews and of Jesus and the disciples. In this chapter we will first consider the potential problems of religion, including some contemporary examples in Roman Catholicism. Then we will concentrate on the need to deal with those problems through reform and renewal.

Corrupting Trends

We begin by looking at ways in which religion can go astray. As Gregory Baum shows in *Religion and Alienation*, the Bible itself offers a critique of religion. Baum's point is simple: The Bible not only tells us of the beginnings of religions (as we have seen with Moses and Jesus), it also warns about how religion can become twisted. Baum especially relies on the preaching of the prophets and of Jesus in describing five corrupting trends in religion.

Idolatry

The first corruption of religion is *idolatry*. Again and again the prophets warned Israel against this fundamental break in the covenant relationship. From the very beginning, the people were always tempted to drift away from the one God and to worship the gods of other nations; at the very foot of Sinai the Hebrews made a golden calf to worship while Moses was away (see Exodus 32:1-35). While this scene may symbolize idolatry, the reality can be expressed in many other ways. The prophets constantly warned against practicing proper religious ceremonies but, at the same time, oppressing people, especially those who had no one to care for them (widows, orphans and foreigners). In the New Testament we hear about making money or power or pleasure into gods. Few of us today are tempted to worship golden calves; but we may well be tempted to make money our most important value.

Baum, however, pushes beyond golden calves and money to warn that religion itself can become an idol when it presents itself as an end rather than a means to God. Baum is especially concerned about idolatry in the Roman Catholic Church (although, like all the corrupting trends, idolatry can be found in all religions). In the 20th century idolatry may be seen in the Catholic Church's tendency to regard its teaching and its hierarchy as absolute, to place inordinate emphasis on the power and ultimacy of authority and on the corresponding obligation for members of the Church to obey blindly.

Superstition

The second danger is *superstition*. Again, there is a fundamental lie involved: As idolatry makes something finite—whether money or power or religion—an ultimate value, so superstition invests something ordinary or even worthless with saving power. All sorts of magical practices have been used to ward off evil or to produce good. Such superstition demonstrates a basic fear and a lack of faith in a loving, present God. Both the Hebrew and Christian Scriptures speak out against this loss of faith. For example:

You wearied yourself with many consultations...;

Let the astrologers stand forth to save you,
    the stargazers who forecast at each new moon
    what would happen to you....
Each wanders his own way,
    with none to save you. (Is 47:13, 15)

Yet it is easy to see how superstition creeps into religion. Necessary external gestures and symbols often become objects of veneration. Rather than leading the person to a deeper—indeed, divine—dimension, the symbol is cut off from this reality as faith slips into credulity. Because religion is ambiguous, superstitious practices are almost inevitable.

So, too, in the Catholic Church, there has been the tendency for popular piety to slip into superstition. Novenas, specific practices such as receiving Communion on nine consecutive first Fridays, objects of devotion such as statues and crosses—any of these can be given almost magical power to save. When that happens superstitious confidence in a religious ritual or object has replaced authentic faith in God.

Hypocrisy

Hypocrisy is the third corrupting trend in religion. We are all too familiar with people going through religious motions for all the wrong reasons. When the symbolic gestures and actions do not correspond to the heart, religion becomes mere playacting or even manipulation. People participate in religion in order to show off new clothes, to be seen in church or to see who is there, to enhance their authority in the community, and for a whole list of other, inauthentic motives.

Such hypocrisy is not a new phenomenon. Jesus, recalling the prophet Isaiah, warned about it this way:

This people pays me lip service
but their heart is far from me. (Matthew 15:8)

Baum also notes that this abuse of religion is not limited to individuals; entire groups (especially those already in authority) may be tempted to hypocrisy in order to protect positions of power. For example, those who exercise leadership may have to fulfill responsibilities such as presiding at liturgy even when their personal religious feelings do not match the public proclamation. For the good of the community these leaders need to celebrate the community's faith and hope; indeed, this celebration may renew their own personal life. But it may also merely emphasize their authority and become important only for that reason. The ambiguity of religion appears inescapable.

Legalism

The fourth corrupting trend of religion is *legalism*. Immediately we must distinguish between a healthy faithfulness to law and an attitude which reduces authentic response to mere observance. In discussing the Jewish experience of law (see pp. 90-91), we have already seen how the law helped the people be faithful to the covenant relationship. But when the external observance replaces the relationship with God (whether in Judaism or in any other religions), then fidelity is twisted into legalism. In his preaching Jesus frequently warned about this corruption (see, for example, Luke 6:1-11, in which Jesus is accused of evil because he heals a person on the Sabbath and so violates the law). The heart and spirit of the law is lost; all that remains is the following of the letter. Such external observance is, in many ways, easier, for all ambiguities are removed, all demands for personal decision eliminated. But this blind obedience tends to reduce the person to a robot; law no longer leads to deeper relationship with God but instead cuts off new life and growth.

Inherent in this legalism is the dangerous attitude of self-sufficiency. Again and again we find examples of religion's emphasis on human activity: some of the Pharisees in Jesus' time, the Pelagians in the fifth century, some Catholics at the time of the Reformation. Legalism leads people to think that external observance is sufficient. They may never quite articulate it this way, but their assumption is that they can *earn* their way to heaven by following all the rules.

Of course, following the law is important—but as a way of expressing one's response to God's initiative, as a yes to

God's revelation. A person can never earn salvation; it is always a gift. Self-sufficiency stresses willpower and personal effort and masks the human need for saving grace. Again, too much emphasis on the externals provides a false image of holiness and makes living in authentic faith very difficult.

Collective Blindness

Collective blindness is a fifth corrupting trend. Other scriptural images used to describe this false consciousness are deafness and hardness of heart. These images attempt to reveal a people's sense of superiority, a clinging to an illusion that they are special. Being chosen and being witnesses of God's action in history is twisted into a sense of being privileged and powerful—and no longer in need of God's grace. Such misinterpretation emphasizes self-interest and denies the need for continuing conversion and renewal. Again Jesus recalls the prophet Isaiah in warning about this false sense of self:

> Sluggish indeed is this people's heart.
> They have scarcely heard with their ears,
> they have firmly closed their eyes;
> otherwise they might see with their eyes,
> and hear with their ears,
> and understand with their hearts,
> and turn back to me, and I should heal them.
>
> (Matthew 13:15)

It is a special grace to be chosen, to be witnesses of God's action in the world. The danger, however, is that this conviction may slip into an exaggerated sense of self-worth, a complacency and superiority which can no longer acknowledge either the need for ongoing critique or the presence of truth in other communities. In pre-Vatican II days such a sense of superiority was all too often expressed in the Catholic Church.

Pause and reflect on your own experience. What corrupting trends have you observed in organized religion?

The Call to Conversion

The antidote to these corrupting trends—idolatry, superstition, hypocrisy, legalism and collective blindness—is *conversion*. The call to conversion is found throughout the prophets' teaching and in the preaching of Jesus. Personally and collectively, people are challenged to recognize the truth and to change their ways and their hearts. People are called back to right relationship with God. The ambiguity of religion, then, gives rise to the continuing need for renewal and reform.

Both the corrupting trends and the need for institutional and personal conversion are found in all religions, in all times. But there are occasions when the need for reform is especially clear. Such was the condition of the Roman Catholic Church in the middle of the 20th century.

We have already cited examples of corrupting trends in contemporary Catholicism: a tendency toward idolizing Church structures and authority, a loss of true appreciation of the foundational Christian experience (the life, death and resurrection of Jesus) with the result that some people drifted toward superstitious devotions and others toward empty or even hypocritical practice of religion. Reform was urgently needed—and indeed happened!

So we turn now to two contemporary examples of response to the corrupting trends: the Second Vatican Council and the continuing debate about authority and dissent within Roman Catholicism. These two examples are quite different: The Council was a specific event, limited in time. The debate is an ongoing process, in part resulting from attempts to implement the Council's documents. Each reform, however, continues to have profound impact on Catholic life today.

The Second Vatican Council

In 1959 Pope John XXIII stunned the world when, after being pope for only 90 days, he announced his plan to convoke Vatican II (only the 21st ecumenical council in the life of the

Church). Such a dramatic event was not at all expected from the elderly, conservative John. Yet he recognized the serious need for renewal in the Church, and so he made his call to open the windows and doors of the Church and to begin the process of *aggiornamento*. Indeed, many aspects of life in the Church needed to be brought up to date, and the damage done by corrupting trends needed to be healed.

Roman Catholicism in 1959 was still profoundly shaped by an earlier gathering of all the bishops of the Church, the Council of Trent (1545-1563). The 16th century was, of course, a time of great upheaval in the Church. Martin Luther, John Calvin and others began reforms which eventually led to the splintering of Christianity. It was a time of serious abuses, needed reforms, national politics and—unfortunately—bitter polemics.

The Council of Trent provided an urgently needed response, one which was very effective in revitalizing the life of the Church. Trent took a firm and clear stance on such issues as justification and the sacraments; it strengthened the role of the pope and bishops and began reforms to improve the education of clergy; it reformed and unified the celebration of the Mass and introduced catechisms for the education of the people.

The Church paid a high price for Trent's rigorous reform, however: The response, while clear, was also very defensive and authoritarian; the polemics did not allow acknowledging the Protestant reformers' valid insights. Trent chose to restructure the Church according to a medieval model—papal supremacy, absolute control of the diocese by the bishop, no lay participation in adminstration. In this, Trent tended to be very conservative rather than creative. The Council also failed to restore people's participation in the Mass; Latin was continued and the vernacular prohibited (recall that one of Luther's reforms was to translate the Bible into the language of the people).

Trent brought renewal to many areas of Church life: spiritual, intellectual, cultural and missionary. But, because of the negative elements, the rigorous reform of Trent gradually slipped into a rigid religion. More and more, Roman

Catholicism reacted defensively to the growth of the modern world. The next ecumenical council, Vatican I (1869-1870), reinforced these authoritarian and reactionary elements.

What was energizing and renewing in the 1500's had become oppressive by the 1900's. So John XXIII opened the windows for some fresh air. His opening address to Vatican II set the tone for the Council, calling not for condemnations but for patience and openness, acknowledging not only the errors but also the opportunities of the time, disagreeing with the prophets of gloom and offering an optimistic and pastoral view of the Church and the world. John also got down to basics. He stated that the great problem confronting the world was the same one that had existed for 2,000 years: People are either with Christ or against him. And with him there is goodness, order and peace; against him there is bitterness, confusion and danger. The fundamental concern for the Council, therefore became the effective proclamation of the Christian truth for the 20th century. John stressed both authentic faithfulness to the tradition and the need to find appropriate expressions of that tradition in the modern world.

And the Council responded to John's challenge! Meeting in four sessions between 1962 and 1965, Vatican II produced 16 documents and a renewed vision of Roman Catholicism. One way to view this renewal and reform is to consider three major divisions which the Council began to heal: the division within Roman Catholicism itself, the division between Roman Catholicism and other religions (both Christian and non-Christian), and the division between Roman Catholicism and the world. Each of these divisions embodied at least one of the corrupting trends of religion.

Healing Within the Church

The radical reform of the Council of Trent had succeeded in part because of the emergence of a strong papacy. The role of the pope was emphasized even more by Vatican I's definition of papal infallibility. Accordingly, the Roman Catholic Church of 1962 was a Church heavy on authority and structure. The image of a pyramid described this Church: the pope on the top, with cardinals, bishops, clergy and religious falling in below, and the laity at the very bottom. When the word *Church* was used, it often meant simply the pope and bishops.

Vatican II profoundly transformed this understanding of the Church. A number of the documents considered the inequalities within the Church. Although there is an uneven quality to the documents, three deserve our attention here: the documents on revelation, liturgy and—most importantly—the *Dogmatic Constitution on the Church*.

The development of the document on revelation demonstrates well the progressive mentality of Vatican II. The original draft, written by a pre-Council commission, emphasized traditional formulas in a defensive and negative tone. After spirited debate, the document was rejected by a majority of the Council members and returned by John XXIII to a new commission for complete rewriting. The new version, finally approved in the last session of the Council, relied on modern biblical and historical research. The document emphasizes that revelation is God's gracious self-manifestation. Saying yes to this personal encounter with God is faith. This experience is handed on orally (tradition) and in writing (Scripture). Both Scripture and tradition, of course, must be handed on by a living community which preserves and re-expresses their meaning, applying them to new situations. The renewed understanding of and emphasis on the Bible in the *Constitution on Divine Revelation* provides the basis for the inner renewal of the whole Church.

The document which probably had the most immediate and visible impact on the Church was the *Constitution on the Liturgy*. This document, based on the vast research and scholarship of the liturgical pioneers, led to the major revision of the Mass. Worship no longer would appear to be just the action of a priest, back turned to the people, speaking in a language most did not understand (recall the corrupting trends of superstition and hypocrisy). The reformed liturgy would focus on community worship—the participation of the people, use of the vernacular, renewed emphasis on the Scriptures. Certainly not all the changes were introduced as well as they might have been, but the renewal of the liturgy began to heal the split between clergy and laity in the most important religious experience of everyday Christian living.

The significance of the *Dogmatic Constitution on the Church* cannot be stressed enough. Like the document on revelation, this document was also drastically revised. Again, a first draft was rejected; and followed by a new document which was more biblical, historical and dynamic. By re-imaging the Church as the "people of God," this final version radically changed the Church's self-understanding. It marked an end to Trent's pyramidal structure (recall Baum's description of idolatry and collective blindness) and the beginning of the healing of deep divisions within the Church.

One of these divisions within the Church was between clergy and laity. The document on the Church stressed the dignity and responsibilities of the laity and set aside the purely hierarchical point of view. Authority was now to be viewed in terms of service. An entire chapter of the document is devoted to the laity. But even more important, its basic image of the Church as the "new people of God" clearly emphasizes the human and communal nature of the Church rather than the institutional and hierarchical dimensions. Indeed, it stresses the fundamental equality of all in terms of vocation, dignity and commitment.

A second division within the Church was between bishops and pope. Vatican I had just completed its work on the papacy when Rome was invaded. It ended, therefore, without being able to discuss the rest of the Church. Vatican II balanced that earlier council in its document on the Church. Indeed, Vatican II's whole discussion of collegiality is a very significant development.

The Council states that all the bishops make up a stable body or "college" which is collectively responsible for the entire Church. The pope acts as head of this college. That is, the supreme authority in the Church is all the bishops together with and under the pope. This union of the primacy of the pope and the authority of the episcopal college begins a new era in the understanding of Church order.

Healing Between Catholicism and Other Religions

The second major division which Vatican II addressed was the division between the Roman Catholic Church and other religions (both Christian and non-Christian). The *Constitution on the Church* takes very seriously ecumenical tensions and opportunities and provides the foundation for dialogue which continues in more detail in several documents, including those on ecumenism and religious freedom.

In the document on ecumenism, Vatican II significantly changes the Church's position relative to non-Catholic Christian communities. It treats them with respect and tries to understand and present their positions fairly. It states that the Spirit is at work in these communities, that they are part of the mystery of salvation. An important implication here is Vatican II's acknowledgment that Christianity is not limited to Roman Catholicism (again recall Baum's discussion of idolatry and collective blindness). The polemics of Trent with its condemnations of heretics give way to reaching out to the "separated brethren." Instead of dogmatically insisting on the Protestant return to Rome as the only possible path to unity, the document expresses concern that *all* parties pray and work for the restoration of unity.

An even more dramatic breakthrough occurs in the document on religious freedom. The classical Catholic position, as expressed in the 1864 *Syllabus of Errors*, at best tolerated other religions and claimed preferential treatment for the Catholic Church by the State. The religious liberty which we in the United States take for granted has not been part of the Roman Catholic tradition. Our experience has been very different from Europe's, which has seen many bloody persecutions in the name of religious liberty.

Vatican II's document stresses the ethical foundations of the right to religious freedom. While the document emphasizes the responsibility to search for truth, especially religious truth, it insists that each person must be free from coercion, especially in religious matters. No one can be forced to act in a way which is contrary to personal beliefs; no one can be forcibly restrained from acting in accordance with those beliefs.

This document, not surprisingly, generated much

controversy. American Jesuit John Courtney Murray, a key figure in its development, described the Council debate as full, free and vigorous—and also as confused and emotional! The issue was not only religious freedom but also the development of doctrine. The Council was concerned about radically changing the position of the Church, a position firmly stated by Pope Pius IX. In the final session of the Council, the document was approved by an overwhelming majority.

Healing Between Church and World

The third major division addressed by Vatican II was the separation of the Church from the world. Discussed in many documents, this topic was the specific focus of the *Pastoral Constitution on the Church in the Modern World*. This marvelous document clearly expresses and symbolizes the spirit of Vatican II, for it is the only document to have originated directly from a suggestion (by Cardinal Suenens) made during the Council itself. With it Vatican II begins a realistic dialogue with the modern world (recall Baum's discussion of collective blindness). The Council accepts the progessive cultural and social movements of modern history and, grounded in its faith, optimistically describes the building of the human community.

This long document is divided into two parts. The first spells out a religious anthropology which is the foundation of many conciliar, papal and episcopal documents. Included in this description are discussions of the dignity of the person, the interdependence of persons and societies, the significance of human activity in the world, and the role of the Church in the modern world. The second part applies this Christian understanding of the person in community to some of the most critical problems of the contemporary world: marriage and family, the proper development of culture, economic and social and political life, and war and peace. The most distinctive note sounded throughout this progressive and optimistic text is that of the Church putting itself consciously at the service of the human family.

The separation of the Church from the world is overcome in yet another way—in the Church's own self-understanding. That is, Vatican II marks the beginning of the Church understanding itself from a global perspective. The great theologian Karl Rahner, S.J. (who had a profound influence on the Council), compares the significance of this breakthrough to the opening of the early Christian community to the Gentiles more than 1,900 years ago. In *Concern for the Church*, Rahner uses the image of "world-Church" to describe this new self-understanding. By world-Church Rahner means that Roman Catholicism is no longer a European and Western religion which has been "exported" to the rest of the world. It has now allowed itself truly to be shaped by a whole variety of cultures from Latin America, Asia and Africa.

Vatican II stands as a remarkable example of renewal and reform. With its emphasis on the Bible, the Council turned again to the foundation of the Christian experience and found renewed means of expressing that experience in the modern world. Deep divisions within the Church began to be healed; aloofness and separation from other religions and the world itself were seriously addressed. Scholars, some of whom had been questioned or silenced in pre-Council days, first prepared the way by their scholarship and then actively worked with the bishops at the Council to help create a new vision of the Church. Vatican II carefully considered the signs of the times and responded by moving Roman Catholicism beyond its siege mentality to become an open and pastoral community in the world.

Pause and reflect on your own experience. How has Vatican II affected your religious life?

The Debate Over Authority

The hope, cooperation and optimism generated by Vatican II, however, were soon to be tested. In 1968 Pope Paul VI issued his encyclical *Humanae Vitae*, which condemned all artificial means of birth control. Widespread debate resulted. Many individual Catholics experienced conflict between personal conscience and this official Church teaching. And, on a more public level, many theologians found themselves in conflict with the Church's bishops. Once again the corrupting trends of idolatry and legalism came into focus.

Since that time the debates and tensions arising around issues of Church authority have increased. Even secular newspapers report stories about dissenting theologians and reprimanded bishops.

This struggle to deal with the complex issue of official authority, freedom, conscience and the search for truth provides our second major example of renewal and reform. Unlike the Council, this is a *continuing* process.

The renewed vision of the Church as the people of God and the extensive collaboration which characterized Vatican II helped to promote the ideal of intelligent, informed participation in the formation and application of moral norms. At the same time, however, there remains a need for official authority and teaching. The result is a very real tension. Some misunderstand this tension and regard it as a certain sign of decline. Others, however, consider this tension to be an unavoidable step in the implementation of Vatican II.

Working out the meaning and practice of authority and conscience can rightly be judged a continuing reform rooted in Vatican II. This reform embodies the renewed understanding of the Church as it responds to the modern world and necessarily involves ordinary members of the Church as they search for truth concerning moral issues. A careful consideration of this tension, then, will help us sort out the corrupting trends from authentic expressions of faith. This very process, then, can help us participate fully and faithfully in this very contemporary experience of reform.

The Catholic Church holds that the pope as well as the bishops in union with the pope enjoy teaching prerogatives of a unique kind. They are commissioned to teach authoritatively on faith and morals in a way no other teacher in the Church can claim to do. That is, the supreme doctrinal authority in the Roman Catholic Church is all the bishops together with and under the pope. In ordinary usage in the contemporary Church this teaching authority is called the "magisterium."

There remains widespread confusion, however, concerning the exact nature and role of the magisterium. In today's Church some feel that proper authority is being undermined, while others feel that laypeople are being denied their rights and responsibilities. Moral theologian Richard McCormick, S.J., who has been involved in this debate for more than 20 years, has concluded that the ordinary teaching function of the Church is one of the most profoundly divisive aspects within contemporary Roman Catholicism. An understanding of the magisterium must therefore be properly balanced and carefully nuanced. Such a view includes the following topics: collegiality, infallibility, noninfallible teachings, official teachers as official learners, and conscience.

Collegiality

As we saw earlier in this chapter, Vatican II achieved a major breakthrough in the understanding of the Church's teaching authority. All the bishops (the college of bishops) share responsibility for the Church, not just the pope; at the same time, however, the pope is the head of this college. The pope cannot act completely alone. Even when acting separately (that is, not specifically commissioned by the rest of the bishops), he acts as the visible head of the Church. Thus the concepts of "pope" and "college of bishops" imply each other. There is one supreme authority which can be expressed in two ways: a collegiate act (as in an ecumenical council) and the act of the pope as head of the college (as in an encyclical letter).

Still another distinction applies to these two expressions of the supreme teaching authority: the distinction between *extraordinary* and *ordinary* magisterium. The teaching authority is called "extraordinary" when referring to the solemn act of defining a dogma of faith—that is, an infallible pronouncement of some truth as divinely revealed. Either an ecumenical council or a pope can exercise extraordinary teaching authority.

Any other exercise of the teaching authority of the bishops or the pope is called "ordinary." Examples of this ordinary teaching authority include the teachings of a local bishop, the pastoral letters of the bishops' conference, the encyclical letters of the popes, and the documents of Vatican II (because the Council did not use its authority to *define* any new dogma of Catholic faith).

At the risk of confusion—but actually for the sake of clarity—one more point must be made: The universal ordinary magisterium—that is, the teaching of all the bishops dispersed throughout the world with the pope—can proclaim doctrine infallibly. Vatican II described the necessary conditions: Not only must the doctrine be taught unanimously by all the bishops, but absolute assent must also explicitly be called for. Examples of such teachings not solemnly defined but taught as divinely revealed include some of the basic articles of the Christian faith, for example, that Jesus is Lord and that God has raised him from the dead.

Infallibility

But what is *infallibility*? The heart of infallibility is this: Since the Church is the historical presence of God's gracious will in Jesus Christ, the power of divine grace (not the human strength of its members) cannot allow the Church as a whole to fall away from the truth of God. Simply put, the presence of God will not allow the Church to self-destruct. Infallibility is a characteristic of the Church, vested in those who have supreme authority over the whole Church. As stated above, this supreme authority is the college of bishops with the pope as head of the college. Thus, infallibility is not a characteristic of the pope's personal conduct or his private views.

Infallibility also does *not* mean that the Church will avoid all mistakes. The Church has made horrendous mistakes; history teaches that clearly. It only means that the Church is not going to self-destruct, because the presence of the Spirit is at work in the community. This conviction, of course, cannot be proved; it is an expression of faith. This conviction, rooted in the experience of the Church and expressed in the Scriptures in Jesus' promise to be with the Church, is validated again and again throughout the centuries in the experiences of the Christian community. The presence and action of the Spirit will not allow the Church as a whole to turn away from God!

Vatican I and Vatican II specified the conditions necessary for an expression of this characteristic of the Church, that is, for an infallible doctrinal pronouncement. Those conditions are: (1) a collegial act dealing with a revealed truth concerning faith or morals; (2) an explicit call for absolute assent; (3) the unanimous teaching of all the bishops.

Thus, infallibility means that the Holy Spirit assists the magisterium so that it solemnly obliges the faithful to believe only that which is contained in God's Word. Infallibility guarantees the truth of the *meaning* of a statement, not the particular *formulation* of the meaning.

Popular views have often misrepresented the meaning of infallibility. "Creeping infallibility" tends to raise every papal statement to the highest level. (Recall the great debate following Paul VI's encyclical on birth control.) Given the severely limiting conditions for an infallible pronouncement, however, such pronouncements are very rare.

What, then, is to be said about all the noninfallible statements, such as the documents of Vatican II and the papal encyclicals? Not too creatively, these documents are called *noninfallible but authoritative* teachings. They are not infallible, yet they carry the weight of the magisterium. A proper understanding of noninfallible teachings is absolutely essential for clarifying the confusion surrounding this issue.

Noninfallible teachings

Noninfallible teachings of the Church are presumed to be true. This presumption is based on the faith conviction that the Spirit is present in the magisterium, guiding it so that its teaching will be accurate. When an official teaching is given, the theoretically expected response of the Roman Catholic is: This is a true teaching.

Still, noninfallible teachings do not require blind acceptance. The proper response of religious submission of will and of mind presupposes study, discussion, reflection and prayer. Such a response takes seriously the distinction between infallible and noninfallible teachings. Such a response also steers between two extremes: absolute submission to authority, (saying that the reasons really do not matter) or denying any unique teaching prerogative of the magisterium (considering the argument only as good as the reasons).

Such a response also acknowledges—and here is where caution is especially needed—the possibility of error. This is part of the distinction between infallible and noninfallible. However, if the magisterium is carefully doing its preparation for such noninfallible teachings, then such occasions of error should be very rare.

Thus, even in noninfallible teachings, the presupposition of truth is in favor of the teaching. Yet this presupposition is seriously questioned by many today. The authority has lost some of its leadership. The birth control debate dramatized this loss, and the struggle over authority continues. Recent scholarship has uncovered one possible cause for today's lack of a positive presupposition: the internal inconsistency in the worldviews and the styles of moral reasoning found in Church pronouncements.

Statements on sexuality and medical ethics reflect a classicist worldview, with emphasis on the static and unchanging, on universal principles, and on order and harmony. Their moral methodology deals with the abstract and universal, with emphasis on authority, tradition and obligation. Statements on social and economic issues on the other hand, reflect a modern worldview, with emphasis on the historical and developing, on concrete experience, and on growth and change. Their moral methodology deals with the particular, with emphasis on history, responsibility and openness to other sciences. This modern worldview and methodology better embody and express contemporary insights. The classicist worldview and abstract methodology, however, continue to predominate in some teachings and so make the presupposition of truth more difficult.

Official Teachers as 'Learners'

The possibility of error means that the magisterium must carefully do its homework. Being official teachers demands being official learners as well. The Spirit's presence which guides the magisterium is a gift. But the Spirit is present in other people and events also! The magisterium must therefore be certain to listen to and learn from as many sources as possible: not only Scripture and tradition, but also theologians, psychologists, sociologists, physicians and just plain people. Such openness acknowledges that the Spirit is teaching in the experiences of experts and of ordinary folks alike.

The possibility of error also implies a proper place for dissent. All too easily dissent is interpreted in purely negative ways and equated with the destruction of authority. Such suspicion is an overreaction, for properly expressed dissent can, in the long run, support authority and community structure. Dissent helps insure that official teaching will not be expressed in incomplete or erroneous ways. Indeed, such dissent may be necessary for the health of the Church.

Conscience

Noninfallible teachings, therefore, do carry much weight and are presumed to be true. Thus they play an important role in the formation of consciences.

Conscience is often a loaded word. How easy to proclaim: "I must follow my conscience!" Yet conscience is a complex reality.

In *Principles for a Catholic Morality*, Timothy O'Connell presents three levels (or aspects) of conscience. At the first level conscience is understood to be *a general sense of value*. This implies a basic understanding that good is to be done and evil to be avoided. (A clear indication—even proof—of this dimension of conscience is the debates we have about what is to be done. Without this sense, there would be no debates, no reason for disagreements. The good is to be done; the evil is to be avoided.)

That is the easy part. The hard part is to discern what is the good and what is the evil. This is where the debates enter. The second level of conscience, then is the analysis of behavior, the search to discover what really is or is not a good thing. Simply put, it is *the search for truth*. This search involves reflection upon basic sources of information in the Church: Scripture and tradition. It includes the wisdom of the ages as expressed in law. It looks for contemporary insights from sciences of all kinds. It takes personal experience seriously. As indicated above, official Church teaching (including noninfallible statements) has a privileged role here, but the importance of the other sources is also recognized.

This second level of conscience is also the level of ambiguity. The individual who acts maturely and responsibly in searching for the truth may still face fundamental questions: How sincere was the search? What sources were taken seriously? Was this really a search for truth or simply a rationalization of what one really wanted to do in the first place? The need for honesty and openness is evident.

Decision is the third aspect of conscience. After a sincere search for truth, finally one must make a concrete judgment. This "informed conscience" must be followed, for it is the individual's best judgment about what is right. Coming to this kind of conclusion is not just a matter of calculating advantages and disadvantages; the process does not fit into a mathematical equation. The search for truth in living the full meaning of Christian life clearly implies prayer, patience, humility and trust.

Noninfallable Church teachings are to be taken very seriously in the formation of conscience. As indicated above, noninfallible Church teaching is expressed in different forms: in papal letters and documents of councils, but also in local letters and directives, such as the American bishops' pastoral letters on war and peace and on the economy. These latter statements clearly do not have the same weight as the documents of Vatican II. Yet they do represent the collective teaching of the bishops of the United States and so participate in the official teaching. Accordingly, individuals must take this teaching seriously in the formation of conscience.

Because human beings are not robots merely to be programmed and so to act, such teachings must be seen as privileged sources of guidance and not programs for uniformity. A proper understanding of noninfallible Church teaching and of conscience focuses attention on mature, personal responsibility in making moral decisions. As a human being created in God's image, the individual has the right and responsibility to experience, to reflect, to pray and to decide.

A Middle Path

This emphasis on mature responsibility seeks a middle path which is not easy to follow. On the one hand, it rejects the blind following of a law, realizing that such a response merely provides a false security blanket and robs the individual of personal responsibility and involvement. On the other hand, the middle position also challenges the casual rejection of Church teaching and recognizes the need to search for the truth and to listen to the wisdom of authority.

The issue of Church authority, conscience and the search for truth is an example of renewal which directly touches the lives of the people of God and necessarily involves their participation. Topics of concern range from the very intimate (birth control) to the global (nuclear war, international economics). Some people want others to make decisions; others would like to eliminate authority altogether. But the middle path of mature responsibility rejects both extremes and accepts the call and the demands of intelligent, informed participation.

Pause and reflect on your own experience. How have authority and dissent in the Church touched your life? How have you reached a decision on debated issues?

Summing Up

Reform and renewal can be hopeful and life-giving, as in the events of Vatican II. But its pace can also become discouraging, as in the present concern about Church ministries and about sexual and medical ethics. As a result of profound frustration, some people are tempted to say: "Why bother? Why stay and put up with all this hassle?"

In *On Being a Christian* Hans Küng, a contemporary theologian often involved in controversy, offers five reasons for remaining in the Church and working for renewal. His insights express well the feelings of many who want to stay in the Church. His first reason is *the Christian tradition itself,* which has provided wise guidance for living for 2,000 years. The second is the *the Church's institutions*, which promote a community of faith and protect individuals from being left alone and unaided. *Moral authority*, Küng's third reason, allows the Church to speak out against all kinds of injustices. And the Church is *a spiritual home* where one can face the great questions about the meaning and goal of life. The fifth—and decisive—reason why Küng (and so many others) stays in the Church is because the Church remains in *the service of the cause of Jesus Christ*.

If these reasons sound familiar, that should not be surprising. They express in different language the insights of John Macquarrie which we considered at the beginning of the last chapter. So we see that renewal and reform return us to the value and necessity of religion. In spite of corruptions and very slow attempts to correct them, the encounter with God and the symbolic expressions of that encounter remain central to human existence.

And so we end up at the very place we began: our experience of God in our world. Whether in nature or love or tragedy or religion, we encounter a loving God who is holy mystery. We meet a God who has been active in human history and in our own personal history. Some find that religion promotes this encounter and helps us truly to see, to have some sense for the profound meaning of our experiences. Some—perhaps at the very same time—find religion to be an obstacle to revelation and faith. But even granted religion's good points, its external expressions tend to become empty, its structures tend to oppress. The possibility and the necessity of reform and renewal are obvious.

Pinching back plants and pruning trees—even banyan trees—is rarely a pleasant or easy task. Yet we know such pruning in the long run produces a better and fuller tree. Renewal and reform often demand serious commitments of time and energy. Attempts at reform may be misunderstood, judged dangerous and even rejected. But we have seen that authentic growth requires such renewal. Only in this way can the foundational experience of revelation and faith be kept alive and handed on to new generations in appropriate and faithful stories, symbols, gestures and communities.

For discussion and reflection:

1) Cite the corrupting trends you have observed in religion. What steps have been taken toward reform?

2) How was Roman Catholicism in need of reform before Vatican II? Did the Council deal well with the problems? Has reform gone far enough—or too far?

3) Read Vatican II's Pastoral Constitution on the Church in the Modern World. *What kind of institutional and personal reforms does it call for? How can individuals contribute to such reform?*

4) Discuss your understanding of infallibility. How do you balance respect for official teaching with the reality of your experience? What does a "well-informed conscience" have to do with daily life?

5) What areas of Roman Catholicism are in need of reform today—in the whole Church or in your local community? In the face of these problems, do you want a place in the Church or not? Why?

6) Return to question 4 at the end of Chapter 1. Does your answer now differ from your first consideration? How?

Theology:
Developing New Branches

Theology: The word literally means "the study of God." But the literal translation is not all that helpful. How can we study a transcendent God? We cannot invite God to give a guest lecture; God cannot be interviewed; God cannot be put under a microscope. At best, we can study what human beings say about God and what they claim to be encounters with God.

Throughout the ages people have attempted to find a more adequate description of theology. Some 900 years ago St. Anselm suggested one which has endured: "Theology is faith seeking understanding." Thus, an individual who is first a believer, a member of the religion, seeks to spell out as clearly as possible the meaning of the religion's beliefs and practices.

In our own day there are a variety of descriptions of theology. Some follow Anselm's lead, such as John Macquarrie. He defines theology as the study which, through participation in and reflection upon a religious faith, seeks to express the content of this faith in the clearest language available. Other definitions do not require participation in a particular religious tradition. Still others deny the need for any faith at all in order to do theology. From a different perspective, liberation theologians such as Gustavo Gutierrez focus on concrete action, describing theology as critical reflection on praxis (practice). So we see lots of flexibiity and no one absolutely correct definition.

In this book we have tried to follow a middle path concerning faith's relationship to theology. In the Introduction, we invited both those skeptical about religion and those already committed and involved to ponder their experiences and to look at religion. This middle path does not demand religious faith, only a sincere openness to religious tradition and a desire to take human experience seriously. Indeed, the dialogue between religious tradition and human experience has been our focus throughout the book, whether we were considering ourselves, or Moses and Jesus, or the Church at different times in history.

Just as there are different definitions of theology, so there are different approaches to theological *method*—that is, different ways of doing theology. As we have just seen, religious tradition and human experience are the two sources of theology. The issue of method considers how those sources will be interpreted and used.

Religious tradition (which includes the Scriptures, beliefs, rituals and way of life of a religion) can be interpreted literally or contextually. In Chapter 3 we considered the problems of biblical literalism. In Roman Catholicism another form of literalism interprets past declarations of popes or councils with the same kind of fundamentalism, confusing the meaning of the declaration with its particular, historical articulation. When tradition is understood contextually, the texts and rituals are located in a historical-social context and the appropriate questions become: "What did it mean in this context ?" and "What does it mean now?" Recall our earlier emphasis on the proper understanding of myth using the same contextual approach.

Human experience, the rich variety of life events upon which we reflected in Chapter 1, can also be understood in two ways: as in need of revelation and as revelatory. To say that human life and experience is *in need of revelation* is to affirm the radical sinfulness of human nature. It is to say that humans cannot really find God in their experience; the answer, rather, must come directly from God. To say that human life and experience is *revelatory* is to affirm the possibility of becoming aware of God in the personal and communal events of life. Throughout our book we have accepted life as revelatory, in our own stories and in the lives of Moses and Jesus.

One final point about method remains to be made. If we understand tradition contextually and human experience as revelatory, how do we relate these two sources to each other? Especially in a conflict, which source is to be preferred? Clearly we have three options: tradition, human experience or a creative tension of both. The tradition-centered option stresses the way things have always been done (whether expressed in the Bible or some law). The experience-centered option puts more stress on the present and rejects tradition if it conflicts with the present experience. The third option is to recognize the values in both tradition and experience, to take both seriously. The result is a process of mutual criticism and mutual clarification. Our two examples of renewal and reform in Chapter 6 demonstrated the difficult but proper balance between the two sources of theology.

Theology is not some remote academic discipline, not some pastime for a monastery. Theology deals with essential aspects of human life—our everyday life! Theology is a task for all of us. Indeed, we have been doing theology from the very beginning of this book. We have participated in a very serious dialogue between human experience and religious tradition. We have seen solid and reasonable foundations not only for Christianity but also for our own experience of Christianity. Religion is rooted in real life not in the imaginary or the magical. Like Moses and Jesus, we can encounter God in life—and then search for appropriate expressions and understandings of this encounter.

Having completed this introduction to theology, you are now prepared to move into specific areas which we have only briefly considered. Further readings about Scripture, Church teachings and moral problems will help you continue this dialogue between religious tradition and human experience.

Summing Up

Our banyan tree really is a marvelous tree. We find ourselves to be new roots, perhaps still dangling or perhaps beginning to root. We are nourished by many branches, the Christian tradition with its stories and rituals and communities. We see older roots, the people in our own lives and the giants of past centuries who were nurtured by the Christian tradition. Finally, we come to the original trunk and roots, Jesus. From him and his experience of God, this marvelous tree has grown. He continues today to nourish all of it, even new roots!

Still, much of our tree remains to be investigated in greater detail. So enjoy your future meanderings through it; ponder all its roots and branches.

Bibliography

The following works were important sources for *Roots and Branches*:

Chapter One

Stories of God, by John Shea.
Religion, Values, and Peak Experiences, by Abraham Maslow.
Apologetics and the Eclipse of Mystery, by James Bacik.

Chapter Two

Man Becoming, by Gregory Baum.
A World of Grace, edited by Leo O'Donovan, S.J.
America, October 31, 1970 (Special issue on Karl Rahner).
Theology and Discovery, edited by William Kelly, S.J.
"Some Reflections on Faith," by William King, S.J., in
    Revelation, Religion, Reform, edited by Kenneth Overberg, S.J.

Chapter Three

The Symbolic Language of Religion, by Thomas Fawcett.
"Biblical Literalism: Constricting the Cosmic Dance," by Conrad
    Hyers in *The Christian Century*, August 4, 1982.
America, September 17, 1986 (Special issue on fundamentalism).

Chapter Four

Understanding the Old Testament, by Bernhard Anderson.
The Word in Time, by Arthur Dewey.
The Birth of the Messiah, by Raymond Brown, S.S.
A Crucified Christ in Holy Week, by Raymond Brown, S.S.

Chapter Five

Principles of Christian Theology, by John Macquarrie.
Building the Human, by Robert Johann.
The Reality of Jesus, by Dermot Lane.
Christ the Sacrament of Encounter With God, by Edward
    Schillebeeckx.

Jesus: The Compassion of God, by Monika Hellwig.

Chapter Six

Religion and Alienation, by Gregory Baum.
The Documents of Vatican II, edited by Walter Abbot, S.J.
A Concise History of the Catholic Church, by Thomas Bokenkotter.
Concern for the Church, by Karl Rahner, S.J.
Health and Medicine in the Catholic Tradition, by Richard
    McCormick, S.J.
Magisterium, by Francis Sullivan, S.J.
An Inconsistent Ethic?, by Kenneth Overberg, S.J.
What Are They Saying About Moral Norms? by Richard Gula, S.S.
Principles for a Catholic Morality, by Timothy O'Connell.
On Being a Christian, by Hans Küng.

Epilogue

"Method in Theology" by Paul Knitter in *Revelation, Religion,
    Reform*, edited by Kenneth Overberg, S.J.
Blessed Rage for Order, by David Tracy.